This is DTP!
A Young Persons' Guide

by Terry Freedman

ISBN 07457 0271 6

GW00746206

This is DTP!
A Young Persons' Guide

©1993 Terry Freedman

Published by:

Kuma Books Ltd
12 Horseshoe Park
Pangbourne
Berks
RG8 7JW

Tel 0734 844335
Fax 0734 844339

Preface

How to use this book

Desktop publishing is something which **everyone** can enjoy and use to advantage, whether at home, school or work. There are many programs available which will not cost you a fortune either – some are shareware, which you can try out for as little a a fiver, and others cost around £50.

The main aim of this book is to show you how you can take advantage of this software. Using the skills taught in this book you can transform dull-looking essays into works of art, produce eye-catching front covers for coursework assignments or exercise books, design tickets for that dance you and a few friends have organised – or even produce business stationery for your parents' business.

If you involved in a project like mini-enterprise, or are the editor of a youth club newsletter, or are on the committee of an organisation, this book can help you to produce documents that will make people want to read them!

The book is divided into two main parts. The first part of the book explains all the general principles needed to help you learn desktop publishing. Read this if you want to have a deeper understanding of the desktop publishing process.

The second part contains a number of step-by-step projects to help you practise the different skills. These projects have been written in such a way as to be of use whatever desktop publishing program you are using. You can use this section of the book without having read the "theory" first, although you may need to study Chapter 6, "Basic Skills", find out how to draw frames, move them about, and so on.

This part of the book will not, of course, take the place of the manual that came with your program, but it may help you to find out what you need to look up in the manual.

The book also includes a detailed glossary of the terms used in the "real world" of desktop publishing.

About this book

This book was word processed in That's Write running on an Atari 1040 STE, and desktop published in Timeworks Publisher 3.1 (Windows version) on a PC. Screen shots were obtained with That's Snap and PCS WinCapture and edited in Paint Shop Pro, PC Paintbrush or Timeworks itself. It was printed on an OKI OL 840 LED printer at a resolution of 300 dpi.

Acknowledgements

The following products were used or mentioned in the production of this book:

Product	Trademark/Copyright owned by
Ami Pro	Lotus Corporation
Calamus	DMC
Designworks	GST
GFA Draft Plus 3	GFA Data Media UK
Hyperpaint	Atari Corporation
Imagecopy	Jeremy Hughes (The ST Club)
Kwikdraw	Paul Schrimpf
Megapaint II	Tommy Software
Microsoft Works	Microsoft
New World PD Clip Art	John MacLaren
PageMaker	Aldus
Page Plus	Serif
PC Paintbrush	Microsoft
PCS WinCapture	Thompson Partnership
Publisher	Microsoft
Quark	Quark Inc
That's Snap	Compo
That's Write	Compo
Timeworks Publisher 2	GST
Timeworks Publisher 3.1	GST
Type Plus	Serif
Windows 3.1	Microsoft
WordArt	Microsoft

All other trademarks are acknowledged.

This is DTP!

The clip art used in the book was taken from the following programs:

Picture and Page .... Program

1.3, Drum .... Designworks

1.4, Arrow .... New World PD Library

1.4, Computer .... Designworks

2.2-3, Arrows........................... New World PD Library

2.4, Speech balloon.................. New World PD Library

2.6, Bomb .... Designworks

2.6, Lady .... Lotus Ami Pro 3

2.7, Ink blots .... Designworks

2.7, Man at desk .... Lotus Ami Pro 3

2.7, Board meeting.................. Microsoft Publisher

3.1, Apple............................... Page Plus

3.2; 6.6, Finger....................... Designworks

4.8, Notepad & pen .... Designworks

5.3, Finger.............................. Designworks

5.6, Computer .... Timeworks Publisher 2

5.7, Flags .... PD Clip Art

7.10-11, Computer .... Timeworks Publisher 2

25.12, Girl .... New World PD Library

26.5, Cartoon .... Lotus Ami Pro 3

I should like to thank the following people for their assistance in the production of this book:

Jon Day and Tim Moore of Kima Books Ltd for their advice and support.

Elaine my wife for proof-reading and suggestions.

John MacLaren, proprietor of the New World PD Library, for supplying clip art disks. The New World PD Library is at:

43 Ingleby Way
Wallington
Surrey SM6 9LP

Contents

Printing _____ 10.1

Projects

Ideas _____ **26.1**

Glossary of DTP terms_____ **27.1**

Indexes

Terms used in this book

* "Click" means point to the item and then press the left mouse button

* "Double-click" means point to the item and then press the left mouse button twice in quick succession

* "Drag" means point to the item, press the left mouse button and hold it down, and then pull the item to where you want it to be

* "Select" means click on

What is desktop publishing?

Desktop Publishing, or DTP as it is usually called, is a system for producing professional-looking documents which contain text and pictures. DTP programs allow you to you make the text flow around the pictures,and to change the appearance of the text, as in this example:

This is an example of manual typewriter text.

This is an example of word processed or desktop published text.

this is an example of desktop published text

In order to do desktop publishing, you need to have access to the following equipment:

* A computer – more or less any personal computer will do, but the more powerful the better, as a rule

* A mouse

* A monitor (although sometimes you can get by with a television set)

* A printer

* Suitable software

A hard disk drive is often useful, and sometimes essential. For example, you can run Timeworks Publisher 2 on an Atari ST without a hard disk drive, but you cannot do so on a PC unless you **do** have a hard disk drive.

You will also need the following software:

* A desktop publishing program
* A word processing program
* A painting or drawing program

Why *desktop* publishing?

In theory, you can carry out desktop publishing on a desk, hence the name. In practice, by the time you've added a printer, space for drawing up rough designs and so on, you're likely to require a pretty **large** desk! Still, it's a far cry from the days when you needed a printing press, and therefore quite a large room, in order to obtain the same sort of results.

What can you use a desktop publishing program for?

The short answer is: anything that you could use a typewriter, wordprocessor, or commercial printer for. To be more specific, though, the sorts of things that a desktop publishing program can be used for are:

* Personal stationery
* Business stationery
* Leaflets
* Posters

* Coursework
* Homework
* Disco tickets

Some examples of desktop publishing

* Badges
* Assignment covers
* Posters
* Newsletters
* Books

What about word processing?

There are many word processors around today which can do many of the things that a desktop publishing package can do.

However, word processors are quite different from desktop publishers. Word processors are basically text **handlers**. They're ideal for typing in text, swapping bits around, searching for certain bits of text (known as "strings") and replacing them with others, checking the document for spelling, words used and grammar... In other words, word processors are used for... processing words!

Desktop publishers, on the other hand, are intended for **formatting** text (and graphics), for example by having different styles and sizes of typefaces (known as "fonts" or "founts"), several columns and pictures.

Word processing and desktop publishing go very well together: a very good way of working is to type the text in a word processor first and desktop publish it afterwards, once you've arranged it exactly how you want. Of course, if there isn't much text, for example in a ticket or a poster, you may as well type it straight into the desktop publishing program.

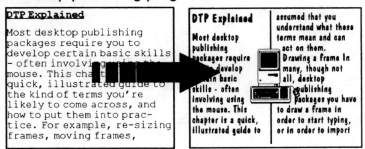

From typing to desktop publishing.

What does desktop publishing involve?

There are a number of stages involved in the desktop publishing process. That isn't to say that everyone carries them out to the letter every time they want to do some desktop publishing: quite often, a person will just get straight on to the computer and work on a trial and error basis.

That's definitely a more spontaneous approach, but it can also lead to a lot of time being wasted.

Over the page is a very structured version of the desktop publishing process, which you can adapt to your own needs as you become more skilled and confident.

The DTP Process

1 Consider what needs to be done, for whom, why, and by when.

2 Design the layout. ie, work out how the document should look, where the pictures (if any) should go, and so on.

3 Set up the pages with margins, text frames and any other frames. (See Chapter 3 for an explanation of what frames are).

4 Import the text and place it in the document, or type it in directly.

5 Import the pictures and place them in the document.

Change the text styles and fonts, and reformat the document, if necessary.

 Save the document and, possibly, the style sheet or template.

 Print the document.

The text can be typed in directly or "imported", ie brought in, from a word processed file.

The picture will have to be created beforehand, and then "imported", ie brought into the document.

This is, as you can see, a fairly logical approach. Of course, it doesn't usually work out so neatly in practice.

Take, for example, stage 2, in which you decide what the layout of the document is going to be. You can take the planning of this only so far: there comes a point where you simply have to get on with desktop publishing the document and see what it looks like, and make adjustments if necessary. (Adjustments are **always** necessary!).

Incidentally, printing the document is a **part** of the process, not just the **end** of it. At various stages – after stage 2, for instance – you'll probably want to obtain a rough printout (known as a "draft") in order to check the appearance of the document.

At a later stage you may want to obtain another draft printout, this time to check whether the graphics look OK, or to proof read the text again. It is often much easier to check a document when it's on paper than when it's on the screen.

The first stage, considering the layout, is quite a large thing in itself. It requires you to answer these sorts of questions:

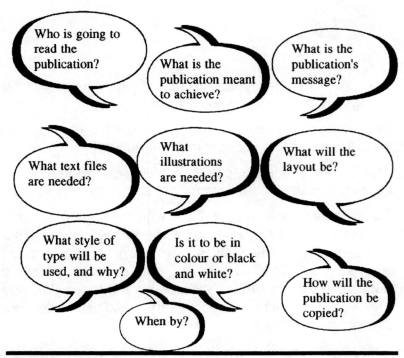

The Design Brief

All of these questions taken together make up what is known as the design brief: a set of instructions or guidelines that help you to produce the best possible publication. Each of these main questions leads to more questions:

Who is going to read it?

How old are they? Are they female or male? Are they teachers or pupils? Members or non-members? The kind of words you use, the pictures included, and even the typeface (or "font") itself could be different, depending on your answers to these questions.

What is the publication intended to achieve?

To shock? To inform? To enlist the reader's support?

What the publication's message?

The same information may be conveyed in different formats depending on the purpose of the publication.

A publication with lots of boxes, graphics and fonts – in other words a publication which appears very "busy" – will give a different impression to one which is plain and simple.

"Hidden" messages are given by the layout, the choice of fonts, the general layout - every aspect of the document's appearance, in fact.

As an example of this, look at the illustrations over the page. The same text was used in all cases, but the typefaces and the overall layouts differ. How does that fact change the impression created in each case?

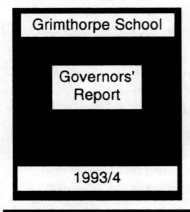

Grimthorpe School

Governors'
Report

1993/4

Grimthorpe School

Governors' Report

1993/4

GRIMTHORPE

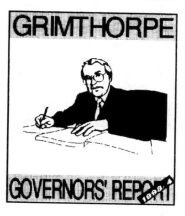

GOVERNORS' REPORT

grimthorpe school

governors' report

1993/4

Grimthorpe School

Governors' Report
1993/4

Which of these 8 covers – if any – do you consider suitable, and why? Are any of them inappropriate in any way? Are any of them racist, sexist, or otherwise insulting?

What text files are needed?

It's important to make a list of what text files will be needed and make sure they're handy. If you're not writing or word processing the files yourself, you may need to make sure that the person who is knows how to save the text files in the correct format - usually ASCII. (See Chapter 4).

Text files may be being prepared by different people. Have they been given a deadline by which to have the files ready? (Work backwards from your own deadline, and allow a good margin of error).

Where are the text files stored? What are they called? It will be a great help to you if the names of the text files bear some relation to the publication itself. For example, "MAGAZIN1.TXT", for the first article of your magazine is more useful than "FRED1.TXT". Similarly, if all relevant files are saved on the same disk, or in the same directory or folder on the hard disk, your job will be much easier than if they're scattered all over the place. **(But make sure you have backups stored elsewhere!)**

Up to now, it has been assumed that there's team work involved. However, even if you are working on your own these considerations still apply. For a long piece of text, ie more than an A4 page, it's much more efficient to word process the document first, and **then** desktop publish it, rather than typing directly into the desktop publisher. Why? Because not only is it faster, but also you can take advantage of the (usually) superior text-handling facilities of your word processor.

A bit of careful planning can make the whole desktop publishing process much smoother than it otherwise could be. For example, you may find it quicker to leave out the title of the publication from your word processed file, so that you can type it straight into a special "frame" or box. (Explained in Chapter 3).

What illustrations are needed?

Similar considerations apply to image files as to text files, plus a few additional ones:

* Do the graphics depend on the text or other files?

For instance, are the graphs produced from data stored on files elsewhere? If so, you will need to have the data before you can produce the drawing. Also, if the figures change, the drawing will need to be changed. (It is possible to make that happen automatically with most Windows-based programs).

* What form will the images take?

For example, will they be on disk or on paper? If the latter, are they going to be pasted in or scanned in?

* Are the graphics being prepared by someone else, not yourself?

If so, do **they** know what the deadlines are? Graphics are covered in more detail in Chapter 5.

What will the layout be?

This is covered in Chapter 3, in the sections on style sheets and master pages. It refers to considerations like the size of the paper to be used, and whether the pages are going to be all the same, or different between left and right pages.

Taking the question of page size first, there are several factors that may have to be considered.

For example, if you are producing an A5-size leaflet, you might consider desktop publishing it on an A4-size page layout with landscape orientation, ie with the longer edges along the top and bottom and the shorter edges at the sides. Sometimes, there are certain conventions to consider. For example, essays/reports are usually produced on A4 paper, whereas computer manuals are usually produced on the United States equivalent of A5 paper. Sometimes, you may want to work on an A4 page layout, and then reduce or enlarge the finished document in a photocopier.

What style of type will be used, and why?

This relates to the points made earlier about the message conveyed by the publication. Different typefaces convey different messages. This is explained in more detail in Chapter 7, but for now have a look at the illustrations given earlier and ask yourself, once again, how the change in typefaces changes the message conveyed by the publication.

What about the printing?

* Is it to be in colour or black and white?

If in colour, does the print have to be in colour, or can you get by with having coloured paper?

* What type of paper?
* Final printout or draft printout?

How will the publication be copied?

This is very important, because it can affect the way you make the document look. Suppose, for example, the document is to be copied, or "reproduced" as it's known, by offset litho. A problem that can occur with this method is that if there is too much black on the page, the offset litho machine can over-ink it, with the result that even areas that were supposed to be clear come out black, and/or sharp black lines become fudged.

See the person who'll be doing the reproduction of the document as early as possible to find out what difficulties, if any, could arise. Another reason for seeing the reprographics person is to find out how long they will need to complete the work. This, of course, will have an effect on the deadlines you set for other people's work.

When by?

Don't forget – whatever deadlines you've been given will have an effect on the deadlines **you** set for other people. You may also need to take into account the time required for distribution of the publication – for example, a couple of days for postal delivery.

Other people

People who don't know much about desktop publishing tend to think it's easy. Because of this they give vague instructions and impossible deadlines.

You can help them to be more specific in stating their requirements by having examples of work to show them. Then you can say things like "Do you want it to look like **this**, or like **this**?". Every time you complete a desktop publishing assignment, keep a copy for yourself (if you can). In that way you'll build up a portfolio of examples which you can use in the way suggested.

Even if the only person giving the orders and setting the deadlines is you, you can still learn a lot from all that's been said. Think carefully about the effect you want to achieve, and do not underestimate how long it might take you to achieve them.

So much, then, for the planning side of desktop publishing. What about the way you actually **use** a desktop publishing package? That's the subject of the following chapter.

How DTP packages work: basic principles

There are two types of desktop publishing program: those which make use of a device called a frame, and those which do not make use of frames.

Frame-based programs

A frame is a box into which you place text or a picture. Usually, in order to place text or graphics on the page you must draw a frame first, although sometimes the program will do this for you automatically.

Once the text or graphic is in a frame you can move the frame – and therefore its contents – about, either within a single page or between pages in a docu-ment. Some packages let you move the frames about between documents too.

A frame-based program. The picture and the text are in different frames. Note the black squares around the picture, indicating that the frame has been selected and can now be moved around... (See Ch.6).

Non-frame programs

Many desktop publishing packages nowadays do not use frames as such,

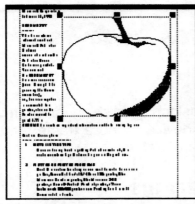

...Now the picture has been moved simply by moving the frame containing it.

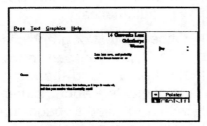

Here there are no frames as such – although they are created automatically when you wish to move something.

but allow you to type directly onto the page.

In these programs, you can place the text or picture anywhere you like on the page straight away. If you decide to move it later on, you simply point to the block of text or the graphic with the mouse, press and hold the left mouse button, and move it to where you want it. When you carry out this operation, a frame automatically forms around the text or the graphic.

Which type of package is better? The two most widely used systems in commerce and industry – Pagemaker and Quark – use a non-frame system and a frame system respectively. This would seem to suggest that neither system is better than the other.

All desktop publishing packages have certain common principles. These common elements are:

* Style sheets
* Master pages
* Importing
* Exporting

Style sheets (or templates)

A style sheet is a set of instructions which tells the desktop publishing program how to lay out your documents. For example, you may want all of your publications to have two columns of text on each page. To save yourself the bother of having to set up this layout every time you start a new document, you need do it only once, as a style sheet. Then, every time you start a new document, you instruct the program to use that style sheet as the basis for the document's layout.

You may wish to have several style sheets for different types of document, eg essays, cover sheets, posters, tickets and so on.

As well as saving you time and trouble, style sheets also help to ensure that the appearance of your documents is fairly consistent. This is quite important in the business world, where companies develop their own "house style".

Some desktop publishing packages do not use style sheets as such, but have a facility for saving layouts. It amounts to the same thing: when starting a new document, instead of loading a style sheet, you load a layout instead.

Style sheets usually contain details of the master page(s) too...

Master pages

Just as style sheets control the overall appearance of a document or several documents, so master pages govern the layout of pages **within** a document.

For example, if you want the pages to be numbered, with the page number appearing in the same place on each page, you will probably need to set this up on the master page(s). Because all subsequent pages are copies of the master page(s), the page number will come out in the same position on every page.

You can have just one master page for a document, in which case all the pages will look the same, or **two** master pages – one for left (even-numbered) pages and one for right (odd-numbered) pages.

Master pages contain details of the headers and footers. A header is a piece of text which appears at the **top** of each page, while a footer is a piece of text appearing at the **bottom** of each page. For example, in this book the left header is the book's title, the right header is the current chapter's title (or part of it) and the footer is the chapter and page number.

In some desktop publishing packages the term "master page" is not actually used. In these cases, look for a facility for saving individual pages within a document, or for saving templates. The basic idea is exactly the same, but instead of loading a previously-saved layout when starting a new document, you load a previously-saved page instead.

Importing

The concept of importing is central to desktop publishing. Desktop publishing itself is really a kind of document formatting factory. You "feed" it raw materials in the form of text and graphics, and the finished product comes out at the other end.

This act of bringing in text and/or graphics which were created within some other program is known as "importing".

Exporting

This is the opposite of importing. It is where work done in the desktop publishing program is saved in a form which can be read by another program, or inserted into another document.

Suppose you typed some text directly into the desktop publishing program, and then decided to edit it in a word processor.

Style sheets and master pages

Style sheets contain details of:

– page format, eg A4, A3

– paragraph styles, eg Helvetica 12 point bold, indented

– master pages, ie headers, footers, and anything else which is meant to appear on every page.

For example...

You may have a **style sheet** called COVER for your coursework covers. This contains details of the page format etc. For instance, every cover will be on A4 paper and contain 6 paragraph styles and their associated fonts.

However, each cover will be different from the others because it will have a different **master page**.

For instance, the header on one will say History Project 1993, while on another it will be Biology 1994.

Despite these differences due to the differences in the master pages employed, the covers all have a similar appearance because the same style sheet has been used throughout.

You would export it in what is known as "ASCII format" (See Chapter 4), and then start up your word processor program and **import** the text into it.

Alternatively, you may want to save the text in a form which retains its formatting (eg **bold**, *italics* etc) so that you can use it in another desktop publishing document with the minimum of fuss. This time, you will want to export it in a different format from ASCII.

Default settings

Many desktop publishing packages have a facility for setting defaults, ie a set of options that will be put into effect automatically whenever you start a new document.

In Timeworks Publisher 3 for example, you can set the program up to load a particular style sheet automatically when you start the program, to look in a particular place when importing text files, to save documents in a particular place and to save automatically at intervals of your choosing, plus several other options.

Check whether the program you are going to use allows you to set any of these defaults – they can save you a great deal of time in the long run.

Document (*.dtp):	c:\publishw\dtp\kidsbook\
Template (*.tpl):	c:\publishw\template\
Text:	c:\publishw\stories\
Pictures:	c:\pcs\
Print to Disk:	c:\publishw\

Some of the defaults you can set in Timeworks Publisher 3.1

The desktop publishing screen

All desktop publishing programs use some form of WIMP environment. WIMP stands for:

* **W**indows

* **I**cons

* **M**enus

* **P**ointers

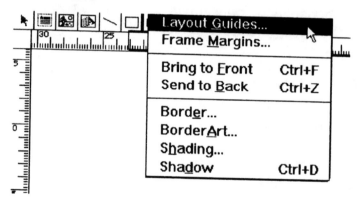

A typical WIMP environment, with a window (the whole area), icons, menus and pointer. This particular DTP program is Microsoft Publisher.

Windows

Not necessarily the Microsoft environment. In this context "windows" means any GUI – Graphic User Interface. On the page opposite are two examples of GUIs.

Icons

Tools are represented on the screen is through the use of little pictures, or "icons", such as when a camera is used to represent a copying facility.

Examples of icons used in DTP programs.

Menus

Another distinguishing feature of a windows or GUI environment is the use of menus from which you can select options.

Pointers

The mouse, too, does quite a bit of work in this system: there are usually at least five types of mouse pointer available in a DTP program:

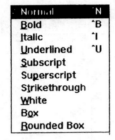

Example of a menu.

 * The normal arrowhead, for selecting icons and menu items
 * A cross, drawing frames
 * A flat hand, moving frames
 * A pointing finger, resizing frames
 * An I-beam, to allow you to type text in the correct place

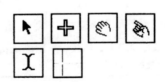

Examples of the various types of mouse pointer.

As well as these, there may be other sorts of pointers. In Pagemaker, for example, when you import text the mouse pointer takes the shape of a page of text, which you have to place in the area where you want it to appear on the page.

Preparing text for desktop publishing

In the first chapter of the book it was suggested that you use a word processor to prepare the text, because word processors are better at **handling** text while DTP programs are best at **formatting** it. (This isn't always the case, but as a general rule it is true). Therefore it makes sense to do most of the typing in a word processor, where you can spell check the document, move paragraphs around, search for and replace text and so on, in a program that was actually designed to all that.

The other side of the coin is that you should reserve typing straight into the desktop publisher for small corrections/amendments to the text, or for inserting the odd line such as a heading, and not for large blocks of text.

So the way you work is to type the text, or most of it, in a word processor. Then, once you've made sure it reads the way you want it to, start up the desktop publisher and load the text into it. This is known as "importing" the text.

Saving files in the correct format

When you use a word processor, it puts invisible codes into the document. These codes contain information about things like page length, margin settings and text style (eg **bold**, *italics*, <u>underlining</u> etc).

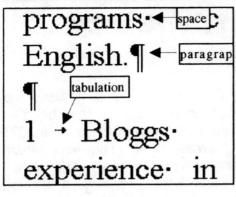

Some of the (usually invisible) codes that word processors place in documents. In order of appearance: space mark, end of paragraph (carriage return) mark and tabulation mark.

Invisible codes are all very well, until you attempt to read the document in another word processor, or a desktop publisher. In many cases you'll get a lot of rubbish in the document – if you're able to load it at all. In order to avoid these situations, you must save the word processed document without any of these invisible codes.

Before worrying about this, just check whether your desktop publisher will, in fact, import files directly from your word processor. If it does, you can skip this section and go straight on to the one on **Tagging paragraphs**.

If you save a file without these invisible codes then any other word processor or desktop publishing package should have no trouble in reading the file. (However, if different computers are used, make sure that the disk itself can be read by **both** computers. For example, disks formatted on an Amiga cannot usually be read by an Atari ST).

A document saved in this way is known as an ASCII (pronounced "Asskey") file. "ASCII" stands for American Standard Code for Information Interchange.

ASCII files consist of the text only, with none of those invisible codes mentioned earlier. That means you lose special effects (called "attributes") like bold type and underlining, but it also means that the document can be read by any word processor or desktop publisher.

If your word processor does not appear to have a command like "Save in ASCII", look for one of the following:

* Save as text only
* Save without formatting
* Save unformatted
* Print to disk
* Give

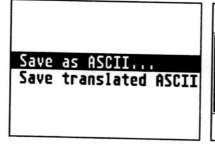
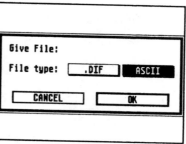

Examples of different terminology used for saving files in ASCII format.

Tabs, spaces and lines

If your desktop publisher accepts files straight from your word processor, you can skip this section. If, however, you must save the text in ASCII format, this section is quite important.

If anything is guaranteed to waste time, it's putting lots of spaces and tabs into the word processed document, because more often than not they have to be deleted in the desktop publisher and then put back in again from within the program. If you think about it, time has been wasted twice over – once while the text is being word processed, and again when the spaces etc are being taken out.

If someone else (rather than you) is doing the word processing, make sure that he or she is told not to put tabs, extra spaces and extra lines in, but to mark such attributes on a printed copy instead.

As an example, if the final text is to look like this:

1   The First Point

2   The Second Point

etc, then type it like this:

1The First Point

2The Second Point

and insert tabs after the numbers once you've imported the text into the desktop publishing program.

Tagging paragraphs

One of the worst aspects of desktop publishing is the time it can take to change the appearance of certain parts of the text, such as in making subheadings larger than the main text. There are ways of speeding up these things within the desktop publisher itself but you may be able to "tell" the desktop publishing program what to do in the document itself.

Some desktop publishing packages allow you to assign styles to the text while it's being word processed. This is known as "tagging". Timeworks, for instance, enables you to tag the text like this:

<headline>The Old Values

There are three periods involved, which are:

<bullet>The Early Period

<bullet>The Middle Period

<bullet>The Late Period

<subhead>The Early Years

(Where there is no tag, the program uses normal or body text).

When you import the text into Timeworks, the tags, ie "<subhead>" etc, do not appear on the screen. Instead, the text is automatically formatted in the desired style. In fact, even if you haven't yet decided what attributes the paragraph style will have, it doesn't matter: as soon as you decide, and make the necessary changes, every block of text tagged with that style will change.

```
<bullet>Paint

<bullet>Drawi
```

Examples of tagging the text.

This technique of tagging the text in advance can save a lot of time and trouble. It is certainly much quicker to do this than to go through the document "by hand" reformatting every block of text that's meant to be a subheading.

What if your desktop publisher doesn't have a tagging facility? You can still make life easier for yourself by introducing your own form of tagging. For example, if you place an "<S>" in front of every piece of text that is going to be a subheading, you can locate each one very quickly in the desktop publisher by using the SEARCH option (sometimes called "FIND"). Simply "tell" the desktop publisher to find every instance of <S> in the document: usually, the way it works is that the first one is found and then you tell the program to repeat the search (perhaps using a special key combination such as Alt + R), once you've reformatted the text.

Dingbats

Dingbats, or bullets, are symbols used to separate items in a list, draw your attention to an item of text or simply to "jazz up" the page. For example, a pointing finger might be used to indicate that the text is continued overleaf, or a picture of a telephone could be used instead of "Tel".

The usual technique for using dingbats is that you load the dingbat font (ie set of characters) into the desktop publisher program and click on the character you want.

However, the symbol is, in fact, an ordinary keyboard character which is interpreted in a particular way by the dingbat font. You can save yourself a bit of time and trouble by typing the relevant characters in the text while word processing it, and reformatting it when desktop publishing it.

For example, suppose the letter "d" represents the symbol ❏. If you type a "d" in the text during the word processing stage it's a relatively straightforward matter to reformat the text later in the desktop publisher.

This may or may not be quicker than simply clicking on the dingbat you want while in the desktop publisher itself. Try it and see.

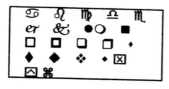

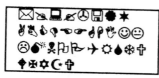

All of these symbols can be accessed from the keyboard if you have the right font.

Spell checking

It is important to be aware of the limitations of spell checkers. They will not pick up words which sound the same but which don't mean the same – such as:

* deer–dear
* pi–pie
* their–there

and so on.

For this reason it's very important to proof-read the document. It's especially important to have someone else proof-read it too: you **know** what the document should say, and the mind has a way of filling in missing details or mentally correcting mistakes.

Incidentally, you can speed up the process of spell checking if your word processor allows you to create a supplementary or user-defined dictionary. The first time you are queried by the spell checker about technical terms, or about names, don't simply tell the spell checker that it's not a mistake – save the word in the supplementary dictionary. That way, future occurrences of a word won't be queried, thus saving you time.

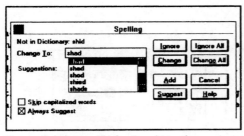

Example of a spell checker in action.

File contents

Think carefully about the contents of the text files. If you have separate items to be put into different frames, save them as different files.

For example, if you saved the page heading in a frame of its own, it would be much easier to change the way it looks, and its position on the page, than if you saved it as part of the main text.

Hi-tec planning instruments!

Where a document has several sections, you could save each section as a separate file. This gives you more flexibility because it's easier to merge short pieces of text from several word processed files within desktop publishers than it is to split up a large piece of text into separate documents.

Illustrations

Just as text is best prepared in a word processor, illustrations are best prepared somewhere other than the desktop publisher. That's because although all desktop publishers have drawing tools, these are mostly intended for touching up existing graphics rather than drawing ones from scratch.

Types of art program

There are several types of art program, which are as follows:

* Painting programs
* Drawing programs
* Illustration programs
* Computer-Aided Design (CAD) programs
* Business Graphics Programs

Painting programs

These are useful for freehand drawing. They can be used for producing cartoons for illustrating a newsletter, an illustration for a poster, decorative borders for invitations, and so on. They are not really suitable for technical drawings, because they don't have the sophisticated measurement and drawing tools that CAD – ie Computer-Aided Design – programs contain.

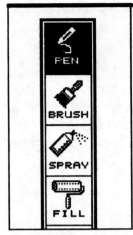

Some of the functions available in a standard painting program.

Two examples of graphics creation in a painting program.

Painting programs store pictures in the form of bitmap images (see section on Picture Formats, below). Because the images are made up of dots (picture elements or pixels), enlarging them can lead to a loss of sharpness or "resolution". This shows up as jagged edges on diagonal lines, known as the staircase effect or the "jaggies". It is therefore a good idea to

Example of "jaggies".

attempt to draw the picture as near to the size it is eventually to be, wherever possible, in order to avoid having to enlarge the image later on.

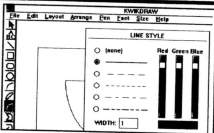

The type of options available in drawing programs. Note how most of the facilities down the left hand side are for drawing various geometrical shapes.

Drawing programs

These are designed for drawing geometric shapes, and can be quite useful for producing technical drawings such as house design, or charts such as flowcharts. If the drawings can be saved as vector graphics (see Picture formats, below), they can be enlarged without suffering from the jaggies.

Illustration programs

These are programs which enable you to "touch up" graphics produced in other programs, including scanned photographs sometimes. They also allow you to stretch, rotate and otherwise manipulate the image, thereby giving you access to a wide range of special effects.

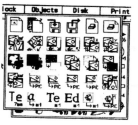

Just some of the options available in a high-powered illustration package.

CAD programs

These are highly specialised drawing packages. They allow you to have several layers of a graphic, change

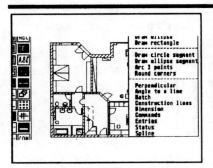

Some of the facilities available in the typical CAD package.

the angle of view, specify precise measurements and many other facilities. They are very useful for producing technical drawings of cars, or architectural plans, and so on.

Business graphics programs

These enable you to create charts for business purposes, such as inclusion in a report or for use in business presentations. You can usually create the chart directly from the figures in a spreadsheet or database.

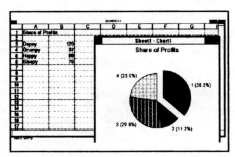

The pie chart was generated directly from the spreadsheet. It could be imported into a DTP document, or touched up in an art package first.

Picture formats

There are several ways a computer stores pictures. These different ways are called "picture file formats".

That's quite important to know, because if you've already got a fantastic art package you'll want to make sure that any desktop publishing package you buy can import graphics from it. (Unfortunately, there isn't a graphics version of ASCII format).

On the other hand, if you already have a desktop publishing package, make sure that any art package you buy can save pictures in a format that your desktop publishing program can understand.

As it happens, there are programs available which you can use to convert pictures from one format to another. So if you have already acquired an art program and a desktop publishing program, and discover that they aren't compatible in this respect, all is not necessarily lost.

Examples of picture formats which you may have come across (by looking at the filename extension, ie the three letters after the full stop, as in "PIC_1.PCX") are:

* **PCX** The format used by PC Paintbrush
* **PI?** The format used by many Atari art programs
* **BMP** A format for bitmapped pictures also used by PC Paintbrush

All of these formats, as well as several others not mentioned, are examples of a type of graphic known as a "bitmap". This is a picture which is stored as a map, in which the exact locations of pixels, the black squares which make up the picture, are stored. Bitmapped graphics are to create, many art packages use them, and you don't have to spend a fortune on the art packages that use them. But they can take up quite a bit of disk space, and if you enlarge them you can get a stepped effect on diagonal and curved lines – the "jaggies".

An alternative type of picture format is a vector graphic. This is stored in the computer in the form of a series of mathematical equations which say, in effect, things like:

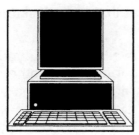

An example of vector graphics.

Line A extends for 2 cm at an angle of 35 degrees from the horizontal. Vector graphics can therefore be stored in relatively little space, and can be enlarged without getting the jaggies. The disadvantages are that they are a bit difficult to draw, since they consist of definite shapes and lines (ellipses, arcs etc), and the programs that generate them tend to be rather expensive.

Sources of illustrations

Where do you get illustrations from? There are a number of options open to you, including:

* ✱   Drawing your own
* ✱   Photocopiable clip art
* ✱   Disk-based computer art
* ✱   Scanned artwork

Drawing your own

...(or getting someone else to draw it for you) in an art package, and then importing it into the desktop publishing program. You must make sure that the art program can save pictures in a format which the desktop publishing program can recognise.

Photocopiable clip art

Clip art is the name given to sets of illustrations which you can photocopy and cut out and paste, with glue, into your document. (Don't be misled by the fact that this method doesn't sound especially "hi-tec". Often, it's quicker and produces better results than computer-based methods!)

Disk-based computer art

This is clip art supplied on disk, so that you can import pictures from it directly into your document. Many desktop publishing packages have a cropping facility which enables you to

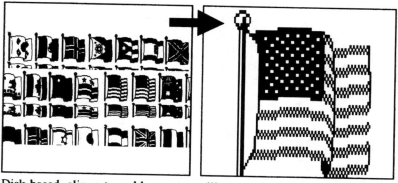

Disk-based clip art enables you to illustrate your desktop published documents with interesting and well-drawn pictures.

cut out parts of the picture you don't want. You can also import the clip art into your art package and change it how you like before using it in your desktop published document. Disk-based clip art is available both commercially and through Public Domain libraries.

Scanned artwork

A scanner is a kind of camera which you use to "photograph" an illustration, which is then saved to disk in one of the standard picture formats. Scanning enables you to incorporate photographs in your document.

Once you've scanned the image you can manipulate it in the exactly the same way you can any other picture. Once again, however, you need to ask yourself whether scanning a picture would produce a better result than simply photocopying it.

On the other hand, you may feel that it's more important to be able to flow the text around the illustration (which would be hard to do with a photocopy) than to have a perfect reproduction of the picture. It's up to you – or the person for whom you're producing the document.

Basic skills

This chapter is a quick, illustrated guide to the kind of terms you're likely to come across, and how to put them into practice. For example, resizing (ie changing the size of) frames, moving frames and de-selecting frames.

As mentioned earlier, a growing number of desktop publishing programs do not make use of frames as such. Instead, they allow you to place text and graphics anywhere on the page.

Even if you possess such a program, this chapter may still be relevant to you. That's because once you have placed the text where you want it, you may think it needs to be moved, or to be fitted into a smaller space. Your desktop publisher may then treat that text or graphic as a self-contained block which you can move and resize just as if it was contained within a frame. If so, then all the skills covered in this chapter can be applied.

Drawing a frame

In many desktop publishing packages you have to draw a frame in order to start typing, or in order to import text or a picture.

In order to draw a frame, you will need to:

* Select the frame drawing tool, or click on the frame icon in a box known as a toolbox
* Place the mouse pointer where you want the top left hand corner of the frame to start
* Press the left mouse button
* Either release the left mouse button or hold it down, according to the software instructions

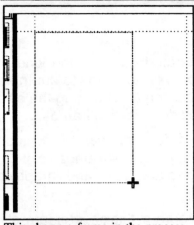

This shows a frame in the process of being drawn.

* "Drag" the mouse pointer to where the bottom right hand corner of the frame is to be

* Either release the left mouse button or click it again

Positioning the frame

You may need to move the frame slightly, in order to align it with margins or guidelines. There are often three main ways of moving and positioning a frame:

Method 1: Manually

In order to do this you must:

* Select the frame you wish to move

(Do so by "clicking" the left mouse button inside it. You'll know when the frame is selected, because it will have a number of "handles" around its edges).

* Place the mouse pointer somewhere within the frame

* Press and hold the left mouse button The pointer will turn into a flat hand

* "Drag" the mouse to where you want the frame to be placed

* Release the mouse button

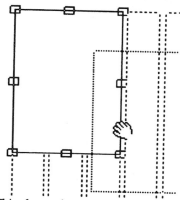

This shows the process of moving a frame.

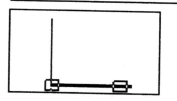

This shows two of the frame handles.

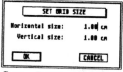

Some DTP programs, such as Calamus, shown here, let you set the size of the grid.

This method is quick and easy, but where accuracy is very important the other two methods are better.

Method 2: Snap to grid

Your desktop publishing program will have options for showing and changing a grid. For example, the grid may appear as squares measuring 1 cm by 1 cm. You should be able to alter this to, say, 2 cm by 1.5 cm, in order to be able to position the frame more accurately.

If there is a **Snap to Grid** option, which there almost always is, use it to ensure that the frame can be positioned only **on** the grid lines, not between them.

Incidentally, the grid lines will **not** be printed out. To all intents and purposes they are invisible.

In addition, there are usually options available to enable you to set up column widths, and to make sure that the frame will"snap" to the margins you've set.

Incidentally, as well as being able to show column guides etc, you also have the facility to show horizontal and vertical rulers, and to change the unit of measurement, eg from inches to centimetres.

Method 3: The co-ordinates method

With this method, you carry out the following operations:

* Set position of the left edge of the frame ; this is known as the "X" co-ordinate

* Set the position of the top of the frame; this is known as the "Y" co-ordinate

(Taking these two steps together, they set the position of the top left hand corner of the frame).

* Set the width of the frame; this is known as the "dX" co-ordinate

* Set the length of the frame. This is known as the "dY" co-ordinate.

Suppose you wanted to draw a frame which started 2 cm from the top of the page, 2 cm from the left hand edge, and be 17 cm wide and 21 cm long. Your settings would look like this:

Co-ordinate Setting

X	2
Y	2
dX	17
dY	21

X: 3.22 dX: 10.75
Y: 1.95 dY: 13.58

Setting the co-ordinates in Calamus.

Not all desktop publishing programs actually call these co-ordinates "co-ordinates". They may be referred to as margin positions, or column positions, or something similar.

The co-ordinate method is absolutely accurate – much more than can be guaranteed simply by using your eyes.

Fixing the frame

Having gone to all the bother of placing the frame in exactly the right position, you don't want to chance moving it accidentally – something which is surprisingly easy to do.

Some desktop publishing programs allow you to fix the frame in position. That makes it impossible for you to alter the frame in any way – ie moving it, changing its size, or deleting it – unless you "**un**-fix" it first.

Resizing the frame

Sometimes you may need to change the size of a frame, perhaps in order to get more text into it without reducing the size of the text, or to make room for a picture.

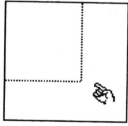

Resizing a frame.

In order to resize a frame you must:

* ✱ "Un-fix" the frame if it is fixed

* ✱ Position the mouse pointer on one of the frame handles and press the left mouse button

The mouse pointer will probably turn into a pointing finger.

* ✱ Move the mouse pointer until the frame has assumed the size you want

* ✱ Either click the left mouse button or release it, according to the software instructions

Sometimes, you may wish to change the size of the frame while keeping the proportions between length and width, such as when the frame contains a picture which you do not want to be distorted. Look for an option to remove all the frame handles except the ones on the corners. Alternatively, look in the Graphics section of the program for an option to scale or resize pictures.

Grouping and ungrouping frames

It can be very useful to group a number of frames together in order to move them all at once , or in order to copy them all.

In some desktop publishing packages you simply select all the frames and the they are automatically grouped. In others you have to select all the frames and then click on a group frame icon.

Selecting more than one frame at a time usually involves the following:

* Select the first frame
* Hold the SHIFT key down and select the next frame
* Repeat the second step

To ungroup a group frame, either simply click the left or right mouse button somewhere outside the frame, or, having selected the group frame, click on the ungroup frame icon.

Copying frames

Copying frames is a useful facility to have when certain types of frame or their contents have to be used more than once.

A typical copy icon.

To take a simple example: Suppose you were producing business cards. The most efficient way of doing so would be to do one, and then, when you've perfected it, copy it as many times as you need to to fill the page.

If you were able to get 10 cards on the page, you could print the page and obtain 10 photocopies of it on card, thus giving you 100 business cards in effect.

To copy a selected frame, either click on a camera icon if there is one, or use the"clipboard" commands.

For instance, in Timeworks Publisher the key combination Alt and C copies the frame to a clipboard, and Alt and V"pastes" it down on the page. In Windows-based desktop publishing programs, CTRL + C is the usual key combination to copy the item, and CTRL + V is used to paste it down where you want it.

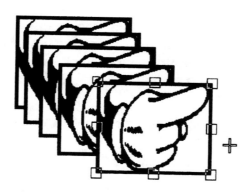

A frame being copied and pasted several times.

Frame stacking

Frames can be placed on top of each other. For example, in order to create a shadow effect in Timeworks, you have to draw a black box and place it behind a white box.

This is all very well and good, until you need to adjust a frame which is at the bottom of the stack: it can be difficult sometimes to select the correct one.

In order to do so you may have to:

* Select the uppermost frame
* Send it to the bottom or the back of the stack
* De-select it
* Select the frame which is now on top

Continue like this until you've grabbed the frame you actually want.

Sometimes you can move the frames off the page and into a clipboard in order to make it easier.

(Incidentally, if some text disappears during this process, it's probably in frame that has been placed behind or below another one, in which case all you need do to get it back is bring the frame to the front or the top of the stack).

Commands to look out for are **"Send to Back"** and **"Bring to Front"**.

About text

The appearance of the text in the document is probably the single most important element of desktop publishing.

Typefaces and fonts

These terms are often used interchangeably, but they do actually mean different things. By "typeface" is meant the design of lettering, often of a particular size, and is usually referred to by name, eg Times Roman or Helvetica. The same typeface can come in a variety of shapes and sizes, for example:

Helvetica

Helvetica Bold

Helvetica Oblique

and so on. This is known as a "family".

The term "font" is the name given to a set of characters in a particular typeface.

Typefaces

There are "umpteen" examples of typefaces, but they are all based on one basic principle, which is:

＊   Serif vs Sans Serif

A serif typeface has a small stroke added to the ends of the characters, such as in the subheadings in this book. Incidentally, "characters" include numbers and symbols as well as letters.

Serif font	Sans serif font

Illustration of serif and sans serif lettering.

The serif gives the lettering a conservative look, and helps the eye go from one letter to the next.

A sans serif typeface is one that does **not** have small strokes at the ends of the characters, such as in the body text of this book. This fact is indicated by the word "sans", which is the French word for"without".

Sans serif lettering has a modern feel to it, and is often used in headings.

What size print?

The size you decide upon will depend on things like:

∗   The size of the page

The larger the size, the larger the print can be.

∗   The distance between the reader and the text

The larger this is, the larger the text should be.

∗   The age of the reader

Older people sometimes find it difficult to read very small print.

Type is usually measured in "points". One point is equal to 1/72nd of an inch. The print you are looking at now is size 12 points.

Which font?

The typefaces you use in a document can help to reinforce – or detract from! – the message you wish to convey. It's impossible to give a list of typefaces along with their equivalent effects: apart from anything else, there are far too many of them. However, there are one or two points which you may find valuable to think about:

* Serif fonts tend to convey a sense of conservatism

* Sans serif fonts usually convey a sense of modernity

* *Fancy* typefaces should be used only in short bursts, as they are very tiring to read for too long

* **Bold** typefaces can be used to convey a sense of urgency

Type styles

Here is a summary of the different styles of type you can have:

* UPPER CASE
* lower case
* **Bold**
* *Italic /Oblique*

(Italic is the serif font version, and oblique the sans serif version, of slanted text)

* <u>Underlined</u>
* Superscript

* Subscript

Some text effects you may have seen could well be graphics rather than text, as in this example of rotated text:

Kerning

Kerning is about letter spacing. Usually, desktop publishing packages come with automatic kerning. That is to say, the spaces between letters is worked out by the program.

However, in some circumstances it's useful to be able to adjust the letter spacing yourself.

For example, when the letters A and V are placed next to each other, they appear to be too close together. Alternatively, the letter O often has too much space around it.

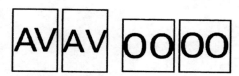

If you do a lot of posters, manual kerning is a very useful facility to have.

Before and after kerning.

White space

White space is the name given to areas of the page with nothing in them. Rather than cram as much text as possible on to the page, use white space to provide balance and interest. In fact, instead of thinking about white space as blank space, think of it as an integral part of the page, and as having as much importance — from a design point of view — as the text.

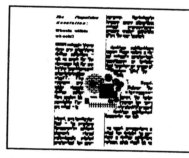
A page with white space...

...and one without.

White space on the inside of a page, with the text flowing around the edges, can be disruptive to the eye, so try to keep the white space to the edges. However, white space around a heading or an illustration tends to make the heading or illustration stand out more, and so improve the appearance of the page.

Rivers of text

These are irregular vertical lines of white space which can appear in text which has been justified (made to line up on both the left and right hand sides of the page) without hyphenation and in narrow columns. Avoid it by widening the columns, un-justifying the text or switching the hyphenation off.

The stress factor

How can you make text stand out? Here are some ideas:

* UPPER CASE LETTERS

These tend to look better in headings than in the body text.

* **Bold type**

This tends to look better in body text than either upper case lettering or underlining.

* *Italics*

This is also an accepted way of emphasising text, but is weaker than bold text.

* <u>Underlining</u>

This tends to look somewhat old-fashioned, and there are more interesting ways of emphasising the text.

* Larger size typeface

This works better in headings than in body text, since the effect can be distracting. However, it can be a useful technique when it comes to highlighting sentences rather than individual words.

* Different typeface

This also probably works better in headings than in body text.

* Dingbats/Bullets ✐•➾✔✘

Points can be made to stand out by the use of bullets. These are dots which are placed in front of each point in a list of points. In practice any type of symbol can be regarded as a bullet.

Remember that text can also be emphasised by the use of white space, lines, boxes, layout and colour.

As a final note, remember that the **more** emphasis *there* IS, the less effect it will have.

Page layout

It is worth learning the distinction between

* Facing pages and
* Non-facing pages.

Facing pages are those which are printed on both sides. This book is an example of a publication which uses facing pages. You can see this for yourself by looking at the positions of the headers and footers. On the left hand pages, they are on the left, while on the right hand pages they are on the right.

Non-facing pages are those which are printed on one side only.

Paragraph layouts

There are various types of paragraph layout, as illustrated below:

* Hanging Paragraph
* Indented Paragraph
* Right Aligned Paragraph

*   Justified Paragraph
*   Centred Paragraph

Hanging paragraph

This is an example of a hanging paragraph. It is achieved either by clicking on the appropriate icon – if there is one! – or by setting the left indent to a higher margin than the first line of the paragraph. The facilities for doing this will be found in the paragraph style or layout section of the program.

Indented paragraph

This is an example of an indented paragraph. It is achieved either by clicking on the appropriate icon – if there is one! – or by setting the first line of the paragraph to a greater margin than the rest of the paragraph.

Left aligned paragraph

This is an example of a left aligned paragraph. It is achieved either by clicking on the appropriate icon – if there is one! – or by setting the paragraph style to left justified or ranged left or unjustified or left aligned.

Right aligned paragraph

This is an example of a right aligned paragraph. It is achieved either by clicking on the appropriate icon – if there is one! – or by setting the paragraph style to right justified or ranged right or right aligned.

Justified paragraph

This is an example of a justified paragraph. It is achieved either by clicking on the appropriate icon – if there is one! – or by setting the paragraph style to justified.

Centred paragraph

This is an example of a centred paragraph. It is achieved either by clicking on the appropriate icon – if there is one! – or by setting the paragraph style to centred.

Text flow

There are two main types of text flow:

* Flowing text around a graphic – sometimes known as text run-around
* Flowing text from frame to frame, column to column or page to page – sometimes known as piping

Text run-around

There are several types of text run-around:

* Regular border
* Irregular border
* Left run-around
* Right run-around

Regular border

This is where the text is made to flow around the frame containing the graphic rather than the graphic itself. The result looks like this:

Appendix to Chapter 1: Basic Hardware and Software Requirements If you're still at the stage of trying to decide what hardware or software to buy, or if you're thinking of expanding your set-up, then

Irregular border

This is where the text is made to flow around the graphic rather than simply the frame which contains it. The result looks like this:

Monitor SpecificationsHere is a summary of the main points to consider when purchasing a monitor for desktop publishing work. As is often the case, there are certain trade-offs which must be made, such as, to some extent, between a high resolution and a flicker-free image.If you want... Then pay attention to...To see on the screen exactly what you'll get on the printout the DTP software To be able to enlarge the image on the screen for fine detail work the DTP softwareTo be able to view one or two A4 pages on the screen at their actual size size of screen

Left run-around

This is where the text flows around the left hand side of a graphic, like this:

this section is for you. Otherwise just skip it and go on to Chapter 2.Hardware This section is as non-technical as possible. It is, if you like, almost a bluffer's guide to the hardware scene, in the sense that it gives you a brief run-down of the sort of things you should be looking for - and looking

Right run-around

This is where the text flows around the right hand side of a graphic, like this:

 out for in advertisements. For the most part, this section is concerned only with PCs, ie clones of IBM machines, although other types of computer are mentioned. There are various alternatives available, not the least important of which is the Apple Macintosh range. However, these others are

When flowing text around a graphic, there are a couple of points to bear in mind:

* Make sure that there is enough white space around the graphic. This is achieved by selecting the graphic and adjusting the stand-off or repel text (or similar) option

* Make sure that the columns of text around the graphic are not too narrow

Piping

Many DTP programs enable you to select an option called "**autoflow**" when you import text into a document. This facility automatically creates extra frames, columns, or pages as required, and flows the text into them.

Sometimes, though, you may wish to control the flow yourself . For example, you may want a text item on page 2 to be continued on page 4. You could achieve this with the **piping options** provided in the program. These are sometimes called simply "manual text flow" rather than "piping options".

Principles of design

Introduction

This chapter is mainly concerned with the general rules of design. Some of the points mentioned here have been mentioned in previous chapters. Hopefully, their repetition here will reinforce your understanding of them rather than irritate you!

Columns

How many columns should you have? This depends to a large extent on the type of document you are producing. For example, an ordinary letterhead will generally have one column, ie the page itself. On the other hand, a directory may have several narrow columns.

The larger the number of columns on the page, the narrower they will be, and so the smaller the text will be. To cut a long story short, as you increase the number of columns on a page, the more difficult it becomes to read what's in them.

So, one of the questions you need to address is: is the document intended to be read, or simply referred to? To give a practical example: a telephone directory would be quite hard to **read** because it consists of a large number of narrow columns of small text. However, it's very easy to **refer to**, because the columns are so narrow that you can read the text in each one almost at a single glance, which makes it extremely quick to look up a number.

This all comes back to the Design Brief: what is the purpose of the publication?

A general guideline which you may find useful is that columns are at their most readable when they are about 50 characters wide.

Another general rule is to try not to have more than four columns on an A4 page.

Dynamic vs static layout

The terms "dynamic" and "static" are difficult to define, and so can best be shown by looking at the illustrations below. Both show a page with a two-column layout, but they are rather static, because the columns are so even.

In the second illustration, the insertion of a quotation from the article helps to break up the text and make it slightly more interesting to look at.

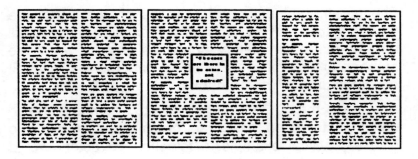

The third illustration, which won't exactly win prizes for dramatic layout, is rather more interesting than the first simply because the columns are not perfectly symmetrical: the first is half the width of the second.

The fact is that a two-column layout does not easily lend itself to looking dynamic. You have to help it along a bit by using devices like:

* Non-symmetrical columns
* Breaking up the text with quotations, other boxes of text, or illustrations
* Breaking up the text with subheadings
* Using lines and boxes to break up the text
* Being imaginative in where you place text such as the title, as in the illustration below.

Three- or four-column layouts can also benefit from these principles.

Lines, boxes and shadows

There is a tendency of newcomers to desktop publishing to put lines and boxes all over the place. This mania for lines and boxes usually develops alongside another affliction known as "dropshadow disease", in which anything that **can** have a shadow **does** have a shadow.

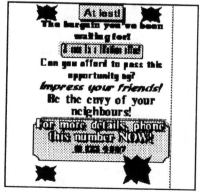

Box mania and drop shadow disease!

The way to avoid going "over the top" is to go back to first principles by asking a very simple question: **why?**

Does it make the text easier to read? Does it help to get your message across? Is it right for the readership?

Boxes are useful for containing text that can be read separately from the main text. For example, a case study or worked example in a textbook. Lines can be employed in a similar capacity – although lines do not separate the text as forcefully as boxes.

Colour

Similar considerations apply to the use of colour. What purpose does it serve? Colour can be very useful for drawing the reader's attention to a point, or for use in illustrations.

If you cannot afford colour desktop publishing it is still possible to incorporate colour into your work through the use of coloured paper. Again, you have to ask yourself questions like: who is this publication for? Presumably, your teacher would not be too impressed with a coursework assignment produced on fluorescent orange paper; on the other hand, fluorescent orange paper may be just the thing for a school newsletter.

You could also vary the colours of the sheets used for various sections of a publication. For example, having the appendixes printed on light blue paper will distinguish them from the main part of the document. Some magazines adopt this type of approach.

Fonts

This topic was covered in more detail in the previous chapter, but there are certain points which are relevant here and now.

At last!
The bargain you've been waiting for!
A once in a lifetime offer!
Can you afford to pass this opportunity by?
Impress your friends!
Be the envy of your neighbours!
For more details, phone this number NOW!
01 123 4567

Fontmania rears its ugly head!

Generally speaking, having too many fonts on a page is something to avoid because it can be very distracting to the reader. Many newcomers to desktop publishing contract a disease called "font mania", the symptoms of which are dozens of fonts appearing on every page of a document.

The following rules may be useful to bear in mind when deciding upon the appearance of the text:

* Use different fonts for the main or body text and headings

* Try not to use more than three or four fonts

* Try to make the different font sizes relate to each other

* Emphasise short items of text by making them bold or italic

* The body text should not be smaller than 9 points or larger than 12 points

Use different fonts for the main or body text and headings

This helps the headings stand out from the main text. The accepted rule of thumb is to use a serif font for the body text and a sans serif font for the headings. But there's nothing stopping you reversing this if the situation demands it.

Try not to use more than three or four fonts

For example, you might use the following arrangement:

headings	sans serif	28 points
subheadings	sans serif	14 points
body text	serif	12 points

Try to make the different font sizes relate to each other

... as in the above example, where the size increases by 50% each time. It tends to make documents have a more polished appearance.

Emphasise short items of text by making them bold or italic

It's best to avoid underlining, which gives the document a "typewriter-ish" feel. Underlining was a good way to make text stand out when there was no other way of doing so. In a desktop publishing program, even the most basic one you can imagine, you have so many ways of changing the appearance of the text that there is almost never a reason to resort to underlining. But once again, you need to ask whether the use of underlining is right for **your** publication.

The body text should not be smaller than 9 points or larger than 12 points

At very small sizes, the text becomes difficult to read simply by virtue of the fact that it is so small. At larger sizes, text becomes difficult to read because your eyes have to travel further from one line of text to the next.

Consistency

Consistency is very important in making your document more readable, and in getting your message across. It means keeping to the same set of fonts throughout the document, and/or the same basic layout.

In a company report, for example, you would not expect the fonts to change part of the way through the document − except for a specific, well-thought out reason. On the other hand, a publication designed for teenagers may make a "trademark" of changing fonts in dramatic and surprising ways.

Even if the fonts keep changing, you would probably want the basic layout to remain the same. This does not mean that each page actually **looks** the same. If you look again at the earlier illustrations in this chapter you will see that each one is based on a two column layout, but they have a different appearance to each other.

A good way of becoming more aware of page design is to study books and magazines to discover their underlying design or grid: is it based on a two-column layout, or a four-column layout? Are the columns symmetrical? These are the sorts of questions to ask.

Another important source of consistency is the way you spell certain words. It probably won't matter too much to your readership whether you spell "recognise" with an "s" or a "z". What **will** grate on their nerves is using **both** forms of spelling.

Similarly, you must decide how the text is going to be set out, and stick to it. If the text is right-justified in Chapter 1, and ragged-right in Chapter 2, your document will not look professional. That's why it is a good idea to make use of style sheets or any other type of template. If it comes to it, there is no harm in jotting down the styles you use on a sheet of paper, in this way:

Body text	Helvetica 12 pt right justified
Caption text	Helvetica 9 pt ranged left

This can be used as a memory jogger from now on.

There is, incidentally, another type of consistency: are the illustrations consistent with the text? For example, an article entitled "Modern Cars" illustrated by a picture of a boat may look a bit odd. Of course, if you did something like this quite deliberately, in order to shock the reader perhaps, it might be a different story.

"House style"

There are two meanings or aspects of this phrase. First, it refers to a **distinctive** style which is found on all the documents an organisation produces. For example, the organisation's logo may appear on all its stationery, such as letterheads, invoices and memos.

Secondly, the term "house style" refers to the consistency of style across documents. For example, if you produce the monthly newsletter of the Year 10 Social Committee, you will be able to give it a house style by sticking to the same basic layout and the same fonts in each edition. By doing this you give the newsletter its own distinctive identity.

Standardising your documents

To ensure consistency of style both within a document and between documents, you can do what many book and magazine publishers do: write down a list of rules to abide by, as mentioned earlier.

White space

White space is the space on the page that doesn't have anything on it. It plays a very important role in a document. Imagine a piece of music in which there were no pauses between the notes. It would probably sound like a mess.

In a similar way, a page with almost no white space looks like a mess. The eye doesn't know where to look first, and reading the document becomes a strain.

Make sure that the margins are not too narrow, and that there is enough white space around pictures.

Balance

Try to make each page in the document balanced. If, for example, you have a bold heading at the top of the page, try to balance this with something like a pictureor another text box at the bottom of the page.

Graphics

Well-chosen graphics can enliven the look of the page as well as enhancing its contents. Here are a few items to consider when using graphics:

* Are captions required?
* If so, what font will be used for the captions?
* How will the graphics be integrated with, and yet kept separate from, the main text?

In this book it was decided to separate graphics from the main text by a line underneath the picture. A lot more white space could have been used instead, or a border all around each picture could have been used. There are endless possibilities. Once you've decided on a format, remember to be consistent and keep to it as far as you are able.

Remember the printing!

There isn't much point in creating a beautifully balanced page if you've forgotten to take into account things like the space required for binding the pages together, or for the headers and footers, or if you've based it on the wrong size, eg A5 instead of A4. These are issues that you will need to discuss with the person responsible for printing the document.

The acid test

There is a very simple yet effective method for checking whether your document looks good. All you, have to do is look at it upside down. This enables you to look at the page as a purely graphical piece of work, without getting bogged down in what it actually says. What reaction – on a feeling or intuitive level – does it invoke in you? Does it have unity and balance?

Previews

Before printing your document you can get a preview of what it will look like. Some DTP programs enable you to produce thumbnails – all the pages in miniature on one or two pages. Use these to check consistency of layout – eg do you always leave the same number of lines after a subheading?

Even if this facility is not available to you, you can still get an overall look at how each page will look by obtaining a **full page view** or a **two page view** of your document.

When you do so, in most DTP programs the text will appear as blocks representing words. This is known as "greeking". You can alter the layout by moving the text and graphics around while maintaining this bird's-eye view of the page.

Proof-reading

Proof-read the document several times, and ask other people to proof-read it as well. If you have a spell checker, either in your word processor or your desktop publisher, use it, but don't rely on it. At the end of the day, your document could win design competition prizes for its appearance – but who's going to be impressed by spelling and other errors?

The remainder of this chapter is taken up with examples of different layouts and page design. Which ones "work", in your opinion? How would you judge whether they work or not? How could they be improved?

Two column layouts

Three column layouts

Four column layouts

 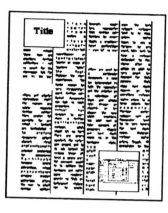

Facts about paper

Characteristics of paper

* Smooth paper is better than rough paper for reproducing very fine detail

* Matt paper is better than shiny paper from the point of view that it creates less glare for the reader

* Opaque paper is better than see-through paper; that's because it is irritating to be able to see the print on the next page, or on the other side of the same page

* The heavier the paper, as measured in grams per square metre (gsm), the more robust it is and the better its apparent quality. As a rule, paper of about 80 grams per square metre (gsm) is ideal for most tasks

* To ensure a clean fold – if you intend folding the paper – , make sure that the grain of the paper runs from top to bottom, not side to side

Paper sizes

Paper sizes in the UK are now referred to by codes rather than by names such as "foolscap". As you can see from the table and the diagram overleaf, the codes are related to each other in a very logical way: take a sheet of paper, cut it in half along its length, and you end up with two sheets of the next size down.

Thus, halve a sheet of A3 to obtain A4, halve A4 to get A5, and so on.

Code... Size (mm)
A0 .... 841 x 1189
A1 .... 594 x 841
A2 .... 420 x 594
A3 .... 297 x 420
A4 .... 210 x 297
A5 .... 148 x 210
A6 .... 105 x 148
A7 .... 74 x 105
A8 .... 52 x 74

Folding

Where the document contains only one or two sheets, folding it can make it look better by altering the layout of the text.

Here are a few ideas of various ways of folding a document.

❑   A3 folded once halfway along its width

This gives you 4 pages.

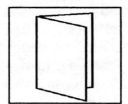

❑ A3 folded twice – once along its length, and then again along its width. This is known as a **French fold**.

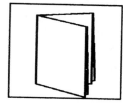

This gives you 4 pages. Useful for birthday cards, or any other document that is designed to stand up without support.

❑ A4 folded once along its width

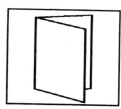

This gives you 4 (A5) pages.

❑ A4 folded once along its length

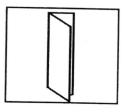

This gives you 4 very narrow pages; useful for inserting into another A4 document such as a magazine or instruction manual.

❑ A4 folded twice along its length

This gives you 6 pages. Each fold is made a third of the way along the length of the sheet. If, after folding the sheet, the top and bottom are on the same side, this is known as a **gate fold**. Otherwise it is called a **concertina fold**. Both types are very useful formats for a leaflet.

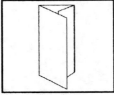

A gate fold.

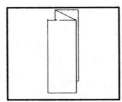

A concertina fold.

Binding

There are several types of binding, each with its advantages and disadvantages. The most suitable one to choose will depend to a large extent on the nature of the document and what it will be used for. For example, a computer manual should, ideally, be bound in such a way that the pages lie open flat.

❑ Perfect binding

The sheets are clamped together and then glued along the spine. This is inexpensive, but works best with thick documents, where there are enough sheets to hold the glue.

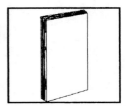

❑   Side stabbing

The sheets are stapled together along the left hand edge. This is very cheap, and pretty nasty too. For example, try getting the pages to stay open on their own!

❑   Plastic grip binder

This holds the sheets along the left hand edge. It looks nice, is cheap and you can add or remove sheets easily. Unfortunately, though, the pages won't lie flat.

❑   Spiral binding

A coiled wire or plastic grip is fitted into holes made along the left hand edge. This is cheap, and allows the pages to lie flat. However, they can take up a fair amount of room on a bookshelf. Also, it is impossible to print the name of the document along the spine.

❑   Canadian binding

This is spiral binding with an extra book cover added. It has the advantage of spiral binding of allowing the pages to be opened flat. At the same time it allows you to print the name of the document along the spine, making it easy to identify on the bookshelf. Unfortunately, the covers of Canadian bound books often tend to start looking tatty after a while.

❑   Saddle stitching

This is the method used for binding folded sheets. Pairs of pages are printed on the same sheets of paper, and sewn or stapled through the fold. Because each sheet contains 4 pages, documents bound by this method must contain a multiple of 4 pages.

Printing

Printing resolution

This is the sharpness of the letters on the paper, and is measured in dots per inch, or dpi for short. The more dots there are, and the smaller they are, the better the result. Best results for the home user are gained from a laser printer, which can print at a resolution of 300 dpi, although 24 pin dot matrix printers can also give reasonable results.

The high resolution of laser printers enables the printouts to be used as draft copies the final copies being produced on a typesetter. (As in the case of a book, for example).

Laser printers are not as expensive to buy as they once were, but the cost of replacing some of the parts as they wear out can be a little high. Dot matrix printers are both cheap to buy and cheap to run, but don't give the same quality of printout as laser printers. Inkjet and bubblejet printers give results which are almost – but not quite – as good as laser printers, but tend to be very expensive to run if you are doing a **lot** of desktop publishing. To give you an idea of relative costs, a completely black printout from an inkjet will cost about 15p, but one from a laser printer will cost about ½p or less. Dot matrix printouts are cheaper still.

Screen resolution

The screen resolution and the print resolution are different. That means that you can't tell **exactly** what the document will look like until you print it – despite the fact that DTP programs are supposed to be of the **WYSIWYG** (What You See Is What You Get) variety.

Printer drivers and formatting

A printer driver is software that drives the printer. What it does, in effect, is to say to the DTP program:

"This document is going to be printed on a Bloggs EX24 24 pin printer. Therefore, to make the printer understand that this word is to be printed in bold type, you will have to give this style the following code...", and so on.

As you might expect, different printers understand different codes, and so require different printer drivers.

One of the consequences of this when using some DTP programs is that if you format a document with one printer driver loaded, and then print it out using a different printer driver, some of the formatting can go awry.

You may wonder when you are likely to print out a document using a different printer driver to the one you had originally set up.

Suppose you were producing a document that was to be printed out on a laser printer which you do not have. You would probably obtain draft copies as you went along, using a dot matrix printer perhaps. When satisfied with the document, you would then have the disk delivered to the person responsible for the printing.

A good idea is to insert an extra stage in the process. After your final proof-reading and before delivering the disk, set up the program with the printer driver for the printer to be used in the final printing. Then examine the document on-screen in order to make sure that the formatting is still all right.

Page positioning

If your document is going to consist of pages formed by folding the paper then you need to be aware of where the pages will be positioned in the document.

Suppose you are producing a 4 page document. The pages are to be A5 in size, formed by folding two A4 sheets in half. The way that the pages will be positioned is shown here.

This shows you that the last page – page 4 – will be printed on the left hand side of the same sheet as the

first page – page 1. Pages 2 and 3 appear next to each other in the correct order.

For an 8 page document, the positioning seems more complex, but follows the same logic. However, a commercial printer will advise you on the best way of organising your document, and will actually do it for you at the printing stage.

Collating

Some printers have a collating option which can come into play when you want more than one copy of a document. This prints the pages in their correct order. The trouble is, every time the printer has printed one page, it loses the information when it starts on the next. Therefore if it has taken 5 minutes to pass the information about each page from the computer to the printer, you will have to wait another 5 minutes when it comes to doing that page again.

A quicker option is to ask for multiple copies **without** collation, and then collate them yourself afterwards, or put them through a collating machine.

Project 1: A simple letterhead

In this project you will create a letterhead to use as a template for your personal correspondence. A letterhead is writing paper with a name and address pre-printed on it. It is assumed that you have set the paper length already.

What you will need

*   Your address!

Skills covered

*   Drawing a frame
*   Typing directly into the frame or page
*   Creating a special style for the address
*   Saving the letter as a template

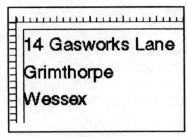

First, type your address onto the page or frame.

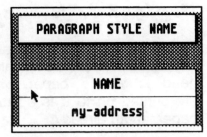

Then change the style associated with that text...*

* If this facility exists!

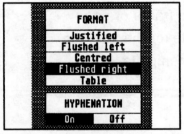

...so that the text is aligned ie lined up, on the right hand edge.

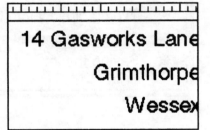

This is the result.

```
|.....|.....|⁴.....|.....|⁵.....|
        FILE SELECTOR
tory:
BLISH\DTP\*.DTP_____
tion: MYLETTER.DTP|
                              D|
     ▓▓▓▓*.DTP▓▓▓▓▓      A
                              c
```

```
    SAVE STYLE SHEET AS...
▓▓▓▓E:\PUBLISH\DTP\MYLET
|.....|.....|⁴.....|.....|⁵.....|
        FILE SELECTOR
:ory:
)LISH\*.STY_____
:ion: MYLETTER.STY|
                         DR]
     ▓▓▓▓*.STY▓▓▓▓      A
                         c
```

Save the (almost) blank page to use as a template in future...

...or save the layout or style sheet for use in other documents.

Project 2: A letter

In this project you will use the simple letterhead created in Project 1 as a basis for formatting a letter.

What you will need

* The letterhead created and saved in Project 1
* Word processed text - just a few paragraphs will do

Skills covered

* Opening a document
* Importing text

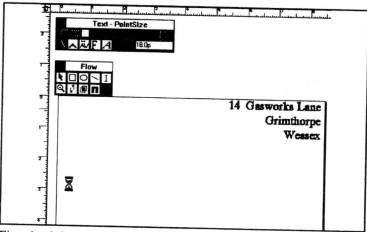

First, load the letterhead from Project 1

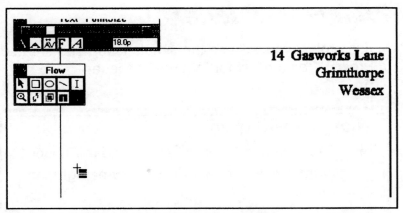

Next, import the text. In this example, it will appear   at the mouse pointer.

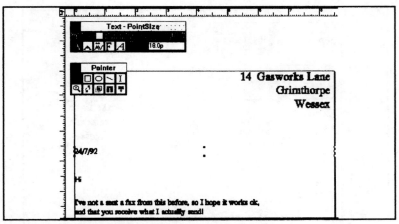

The text has been imported, and put in the correct place.

The date is moved over to the right by using a right-justified paragraph style.

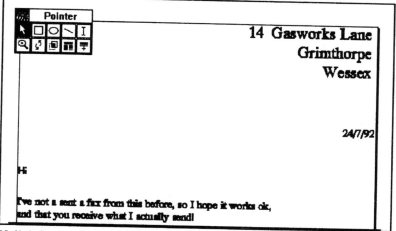

Voila! Save this by a different name, and the original letterhead will remain intact. See overleaf if you use a frame-based program.

If you use a frame-based program you can save yourself a bit of time and trouble over the long run by using a very simple trick:

Put the address in its own, small, frame. Then create another frame for the body of the letter.

By doing this, you will never have to mess about trying to put the cursor in the right place before importing the letter text. All you'll need to do is go into text mode and then click in the main frame.

Project 3: Letterhead with logo

Rather than have just an ordinary letterhead, you may prefer to have one which incorporates a picture.

In the example used here, the graphic consists of a "handwritten" effect which was created in a painting program. However, the principles involved are exactly the same as if a "proper" drawing was used.

What you will need

 ✳ A previously-created graphic to use as a logo

Skills covered

 ✳ Importing a graphic

 ✳ Drawing and resizing frames

First, import the graphic...

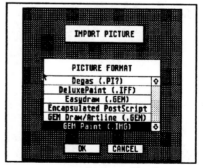

...you may need to specify the type.

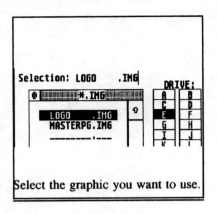

Select the graphic you want to use.

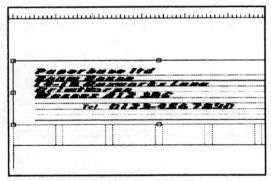

In this example, the picture has been imported into a frame. As you can see, it's somewhat distorted...

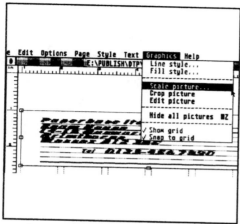

...and so needs rescaling.

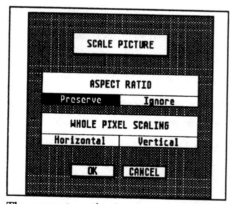

The **aspect ratio** is the relationship between the vertical and the horizontal aspects of the graphic. In this example, the aspect ratio was lost initially. By preserving it, the picture will appear less distorted.

In this particular DTP program (Timeworks Publisher 2), you can fine tune the aspect ratio even further by the use of whole pixel scaling. This helps to avoid moiré patterns appearing in the printed graphic.

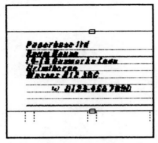

As you can see, the graphic is no longer

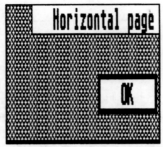

An example of a moiré pattern.

Different programs have different ways of enabling you to rescale graphics while maintaining their correct proportions, such as:

* Selecting a menu entry for scaling or rescaling, in which you specify the aspect ratios manually

* Changing the size of the picture by resizing it while the Alt, Shift or Control key is held down

* Clicking on an icon

* Using a keyboard shortcut

Once you've positioned the logo exactly where you want it, save the document as a template or style sheet. In this way, you can always use it as a basis for all of your letters.

Project 4: A simple poster

A poster is a notice that is intended to be read by passers-by. It therefore has to be quite eye-catching. It has to make enough of an impact to make the person who sees it want to stop and read more.

Let's take a fairly ordinary example – a notice for a concert in the local village hall.

What you will need

* Nothing!

Skills covered

* Drawing frames
* Formatting text
* Using different fonts

The Village Green
presents

The Blues People
in concert

Friday 18th September 1992

Doors Open 7.30

Tickets £5 on the door

Refreshments available

Type in the text directly on to the page, or into the program's text editor - if there is one. (There is not enough text to justify using a word processor). As you can see, the appearance of the poster leaves something to be desired!

The Village Green

presents

The Blues People
in concert

Friday 18th September 1992

Doors Open 7.30

Tickets £5 on the door

Refreshments available

In order to make the poster more attractive, you can highlight the top line (usually by pressing and holding down the left mouse button and dragging the mouse pointer over the text).

Next, select another font. Note that an alternative method in some programs is to make the heading a different paragraph style.

The Village Green

presents

The Blues People
in concert

Friday 18th September 1992

Doors Open 7.30

Tickets £5 on the door

Refreshments available

The font has been changed from serif to sans serif, and the type enlarged. It has also been centred, by highlighting it and clicking on the centering icon shown above right.

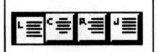

Icons like these make formatting the text a fairly easy task.

Using these techniques, and by adding a little more line space between "in concert" and "Friday...", the poster opposite has been produced.

The Village Green

presents

The Blues People
in concert

Friday 18th September 1992

Doors Open 7.30

Tickets £5 on the door

Refreshments available

The final result

Project 5: A poster with graphics

They say a picture speaks a thousand words, and this is especially true of posters. An appropriate and well-placed picture can grab the passer-by's attention and make them want to find out what it's all about.

In this project we take the poster produced in Project 4 and embellish it with a picture.

What you will need

* The poster you produced in Project 4
* A previously created picture of a harmonica

Skills covered

* Opening a document
* Importing graphics
* Cropping pictures
* Resizing pictures

This is the poster we created last time...

...and this is how it will look when it's been amended.

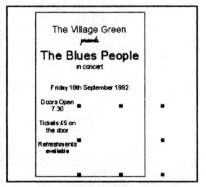

First, draw a frame for the picture. Note that in some DTP programs you can skip this step.

Next, import the picture. This is usually an option in the File menu.

There are unwanted areas here, so the cropping function is selected...

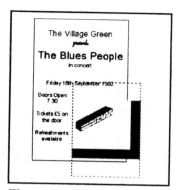

The dotted lines indicate which parts of the picture will be left once you've finished cropping it.

This looks much better now. However, look how the graphic has pushed the text out of the way Unfortunately, it's done so by splitting the words up in an unacceptable manner.

Hold the left mouse button down and drag the picture over to the right.

The Village Green

presents

The Blues People

in concert

Friday 18th September 1992

Doors Open 7.30

Tickets £5 on
the door

Refreshments
available

And here we are! Because this is a screen shot, and one which has been greatly enlarged, the lettering looks jagged. If your DTP program uses vector or outline fonts, rather than bitmapped fonts, this won't happen.

Project 6: Poster with a border

Sometimes you can enhance the appearance of a poster by adding a border to it. This is a fairly straightforward procedure which involves drawing a frame around the perimeter of the poster and then making choices about such things as the thickness of the border and whether it is plain or patterned.

What you will need

* The poster you created in Project 5

Skills covered

* Opening a document
* Drawing a border
* Choosing/changing the border attributes

First, open the document which you created in Project 5 – the poster advertising a concert. It is shown here with its frame selected, as shown by the little black squares (handles) around the edge.

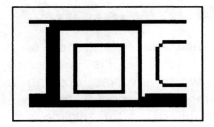

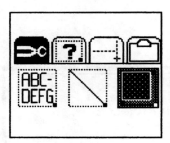

The next step is to select the border drawing tool. This is normally indicated as an icon, as shown in the three examples here (shown highlighted). Some programs, like Timeworks Publisher 2, require you to draw an ordinary frame and then give it a

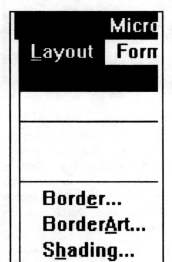

Once you've drawn the border or frame you need to set its attributes. This may be done either through a menu system or by clicking on icons. Both methods are shown here and on the facing page.

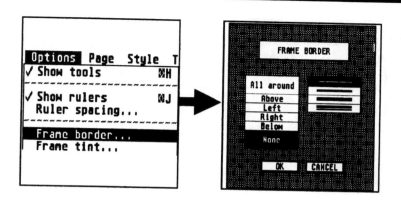

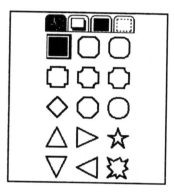

These screen shots and the one on the previous page illustrate the various means by which you can configure some of the attributes of the frame border.

As well as selecting the shape of the border and, in some programs, whether it is visible all the way round or on one or more sides of the frame, you can often choose the thickness of the lines and even the pattern of the border. Examples are shown over the page.

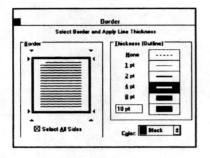

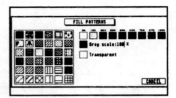

Examples of selection of border thickness (left) and border pattern (above).

Returning to the task in hand, the picture on the left shows what the frame border looks like after it has been made thicker. The steps involved were: select the frame or draw the border and select that, and then change its attributes.

Rather than simply making the border of the poster thicker, you could give it a pattern of some kind. The page opposite shows two examples of this – one from Calamus, the other from Microsoft Publisher.

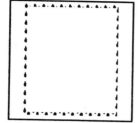

This shows a patterned border created in Calamus. The following effect was achieved with Microsoft Publisher.

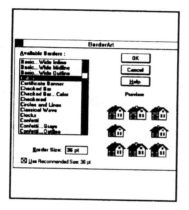

In some DTP programs you can have a border made up from clip art. This can make for a very interesting effect. Instead of setting the border thickness, you choose the clip art to be used, and the program does the rest.

In this particular example, the border art was too large, and so it affected the layout (above). The border could have been made thinner, but in this case it was decided to resize the picture of the harmonica instead (left).

This is DTP!

Suppose you'd like to create the effect shown on the previous page, but you don't have a program with a border art facility?

All is not lost! The next project shows you how you can achieve your ambition.

Project 7: Creating a border

In Project 6 you produced a poster with a border which consisted of clip art. That was easy because the DTP program used to illustrate the project contained a border art facility.

What if your program lacks this facility? No problem! You can still create the same effect; it just takes a little bit longer, that's all.

For the sake of clarity, the illustrations given here show the border only, not the poster itself.

What you will need
* A previously-created picture

Skills covered
* Importing a picture
* Resizing a picture
* Copying a frame
* Selecting several frames
* Copying several frames
* Moving frames

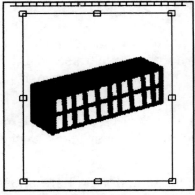

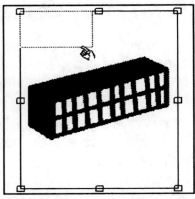

First, draw an appropriate picture in a painting program, or use clip art. Note that a harmonica is being used, since this is more appropriate for a blues concert poster than is a cabin!

Next, resize the frame until it is small enough to form part of a border...

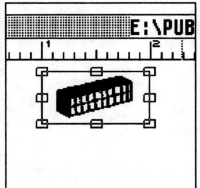

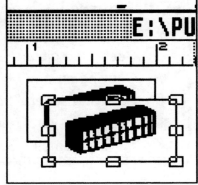

...This is probably about the right size.

Now copy the frame and paste it. There are now two identical frames.

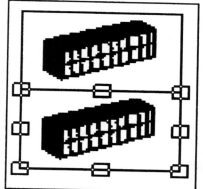 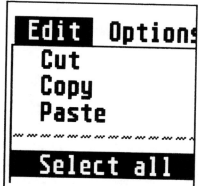

Align the frames one on top of the other. If you have a snap-to-guides option use it, because it will help you align the frames exactly, and get the spacing right.

When you've done this with several frames, use the **Select all** function to select all of them together – or select several by doing it "manually".

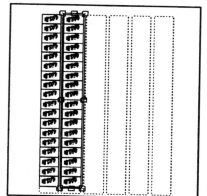 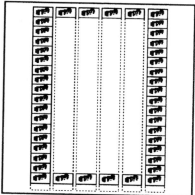

Then copy them all in one go. Move the copied frames to the correct position – all at once.

Continue like this in order to get through the task much more quickly.

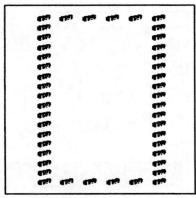

And here is the result.

All of the skills covered in the first seven projects will be applied in the next few projects. These are concerned with business stationery.

The principles of these business projects can be applied to school enterprise projects and to your own family's small business.

Project 8: Creating memos

In this and the three projects following the theme is business stationery. Taken overall, the three projects indicate how a house style can be created over different types of business stationery – in particular, memos, compliments slips, business cards and invoices.

You can use your imagination to extend the concept to, say, letterheads and price lists.

What you will need

* A graphic to use as a logo

Skills covered

* Importing graphics
* Copying and pasting frames
* Copying and pasting lines
* Moving frames

f 🌸 ower

power

1 2 Gravelpit Lane
Grimthorpe
Wessex
01-123 4567

Memo

Date:

To:

Re:

This is how the finished product will look.

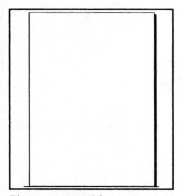

First, start with an empty frame.

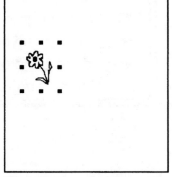

Then import a picture that you've created beforehand.

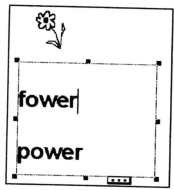

Next, draw a text frame and type the words "fower power".

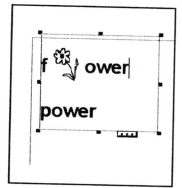

Now move the text frame up until it covers the picture of the flower. The flower should cause the word "fower" to flow around it. You may have to experiment with the "bring to front/back options" though.

Now, in another text frame, type the address etc.

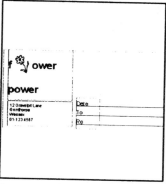

In yet another text frame type "Date:","To:" and "Re:" Then, using the line drawing facility, add a few lines.

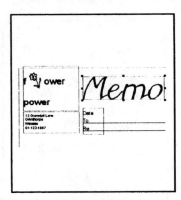

The final stage is to insert the word "Memo". In the example shown here, WordArt, which comes built-in to Microsoft Publisher, has been used. A similar product is Type Plus, by Serif. Alternatively, a separate graphics program could have been used, and the result **imported** into the document.

You can use certain elements of this document again, in different but related documents. In the next project, an invoice is created using the same logo and address style.

If you are using a Windows program, doing this is easy: you just select the frames you want to use again, copy them, open a new document, and paste them.

If you are not using a Windows program you may need to be more resourceful. You may, for example, be able to save just one page of this document, load it up as a separate document, and cut out the bits you don't need. Or perhaps you could **export** the parts you need, and import them into a new document. Use your imagination!

Project 9: Creating invoices

Continuing the theme of business stationery, this project looks at the creation of invoices. It also looks at the creation of a house style by using certain elements from the memo created in Project 8. To make life a little easier for yourself in that respect, take a look at the suggestions made at the end of that project, on page 18.4

What you will need

   ✳   The logo and address panel from Project 8

Skills covered

   ✳   Importing graphics

   ✳   Pasting frames from another document

   ✳   Cutting and pasting frames within a document

   ✳   Creating and positioning lines

   ✳   Using tabs

   ✳   Positioning text

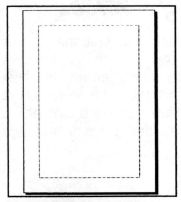

First, start with a blank page as usual.

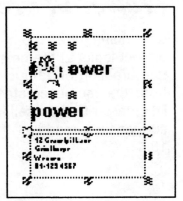

Next, import or paste in the logo and the address panel.

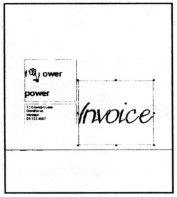

Then create the title "Invoice" in the same way as you created the title "Memo" in the previous project.

Now draw a box for the column titles. Take a copy of this box, but don't paste it just yet.

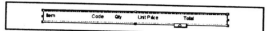

In this box, draw a text frame (if necessary), and type the words "Item", "Code", "Qty", "Unit Price" and "Total". Separate them by tabs, not spaces, and then set the tabs so that the text appears as shown here.

Depending on the program you are using, you will either have to set the tabs by clicking on the ruler, clicking on an icon, selecting an item from a format or layout menu, or configure a special paragraph style.

Happy hunting!

Now you can paste the box you copied earlier, and position it under and next to the first one. The snap-to-grid option is useful here, since it will help you align the two frames exactly. If you can specify that the border of the second frame is invisible on top, then double thickness lines where the two boxes touch will be avoided.

After adding a few more boxes like that (simply by continuing to paste them), the document is starting to take shape.

Then add the vertical lines – either by drawing boxes or using the line drawing tool – and add the VAT and TOTAL boxes and labels. If you are using a frame-based package, the labels will be easier to position if you draw a text frame especially for them.

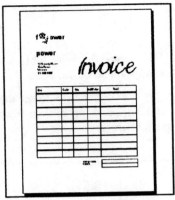

This is how the document looks at the moment.

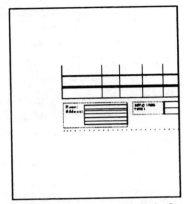

Now draw boxes and labels for the customer's name & address.

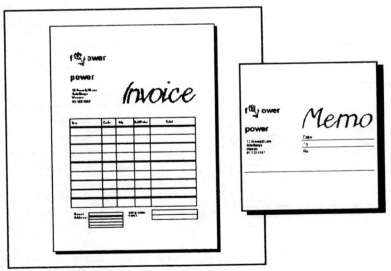

And here is the finished product. The memo document has been added for comparison. Notice the existence of a house style?

Project 10: Creating a compliments slip

Once again, we look at how to produce an item of business stationery. By now, you should be getting the hang of how to do it! Look at the previous two projects for extra guidance if you need to.

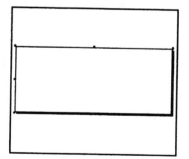

Start with a blank page and draw a frame. Make the frame the exact size you want by using one of the methods given in Chapter 6. Compliments slips come in all shapes and sizes; 6" by 3" or similar is often used.

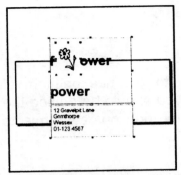

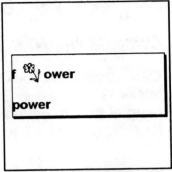

Next, import or paste in the logo and address panel. Move the address panel out of the way...

...and place the logo in position on the left hand side of the compliments slip.

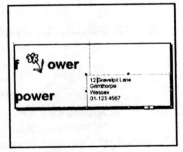

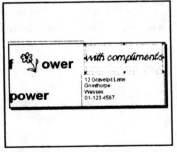

Now retrieve and position the address panel.

Finally, create or import the "with compliments" wording.

The results of your labours are shown on the page opposite.

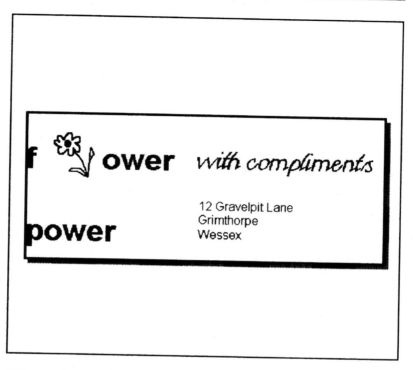

Why not use the same principles, logo and lettering to create a business letterhead, receipts, fax cover sheet and other types of business stationery?

Project 11: Creating business cards

This project continues with the theme of business stationery. A business card may be the first contact between you and a potential client or customer. It is therefore important that it reflects the nature of the business in its style and overall appearance.

As an example, look at the business card below. Seem familiar? Perhaps you'd like to try creating this on your own, because the main aim of this project is not so much the creation of business cards, but the use of a simple labour and cost-savin technique.

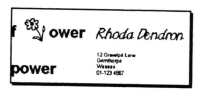

What you will need

* Nothing

Skills covered

* Using the **Select all** facility
* Copying and pasting grouped frames

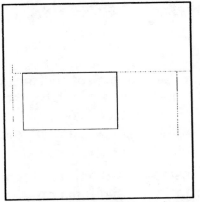

First, draw a box the size of your business card. This will help in the cutting out stage later on.

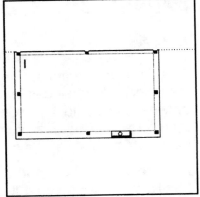

Next, draw a text frame inside the box.

Type your name and address. In this example, a fancy font has been used for the name...

...in keeping with the person's occupation. The word "artist" is actually an imported graphic.

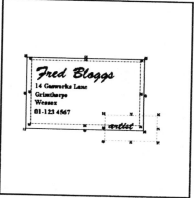

As it happens, I didn't like the graphic, so I typed "artist" instead! By using the same typeface as the name, I have established a link between the two.

Now use the **Select all** function and/or the **group frame** facility...

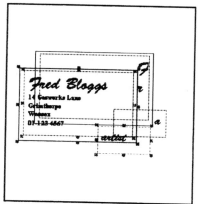

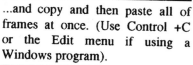

...and copy and then paste all of frames at once. (Use Control +C or the Edit menu if using a Windows program).

Then align the new business card alongside the original.

Continue to copy and paste until you have a whole page full of cards.

This shows the same thing, but without all the grid lines showing.

Once you've produced a whole sheetful of cards, print it and then photocopy it onto card. Use a guillotine to cut the card . As this is quite a skilled job, you may prefer to ask a more experienced person to do it for you.

Project 12: Creating a company report cover

The house style of a company can also find its way onto the cover of a company report. Even though the logo and font styles used in the "Flower Power" business stationery may appear rather frivolous, they can be used to good effect on the cover of a report. Key elements are positioning and white space.

What you will need
* The logo used in Project 8

Skills covered
* Layout and design

As far as positioning is concerned, many people often place the name of the document in the horizontal centre of the page. But why **should** everything always be horizontally centred? In the example given here, most of the wording is on the right hand edge of the page. Also, if you want something to look vertically centred, put it **above** the centre of the page, as we've done here. Otherwise it will probably look too low down.

As for white space – ideally there should be plenty of it!

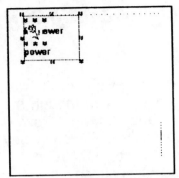

First, import or paste in the logo you are going to use.

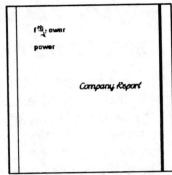

Type "Company Report" in a text frame created and positioned specifically for that purpose.

A close-up view of the front cover.

Move the logo over to the right, using the horizontal ruler to guide you.

Add the financial year...

...and a line above the title...

...and a line under it. Done!

A larger version of the cover is to be found overleaf. Incidentally, make sure that the style of the inside of the report is consistent with that of the cover.

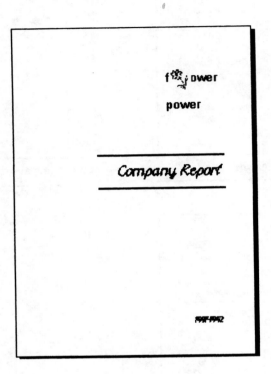

Project 13: Creating a newsletter

Here is a 3-column newsletter for you to create. The skills involved can, of course, be used in the creation of any other document which requires multiple columns, such as price lists, directories, even text books.

What you will need

* Two or three word processed documents — perhaps saved as ASCII files
* Two graphics to use as illustrations

Skills covered

* Setting up columns
* Flowing text from column to column

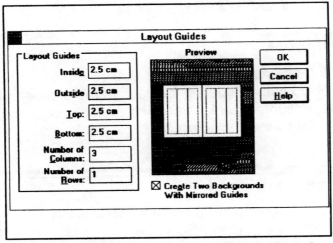

Start a new document, and call up the column guides option. This will probably be in a layout or options menu. In the example shown, the layout has been set to 3 columns, and the left and right pages have been set to mirror each other. That will give the newsletter a more polished appearance.

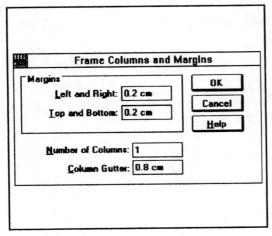

There are often further options availabl which enable you to adjust the spac between columns, and to alter other margins on the page.

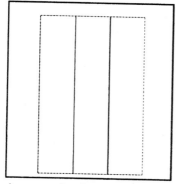

As a result of your responses to the previous dialogue boxes, you should end up with a page with guidelines for three columns, as in the example shown here.

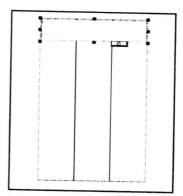

Draw a frame for the title at the top of the page. This should be fairly large.

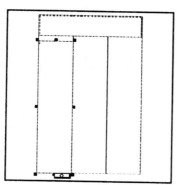

Next, draw a frame for the first column...

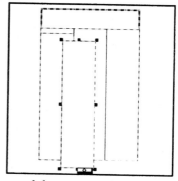

...and then copy and paste it to make the second column.

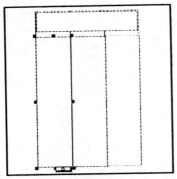

Repeat the process to give 3 columns, and select the first.

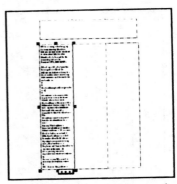

Import the text you want, via the File menu.

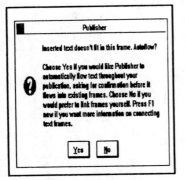

Automatic text flow is easier, but manual text flow gives you more scope.

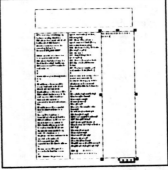

In some programs you have to set up links between one column and the next; in others you select the next column and click on the name of the imported text, which then continues from where it broke

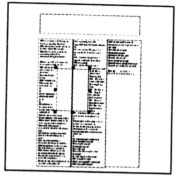

Draw in a picture frame over part of columns one and two. Notice how the tex automatically flows around it.

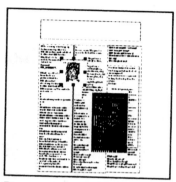

Draw another picture frame, and import a picture into each frame. Now it's starting to take shape!

Now type in the title...

...and enlarge it!

All that remains is to insert the date and price and other similar items – and, of course, a few extra pages!

Project 14: Setting out a book

Setting out a book, or other multi-paged documents such as a company report, requires many of the skills already covered plus a few more. In this project you are going to be introduced to using master pages and headers and footers.

What you will need

* Nothing

Skills covered

* Setting up master pages
* Setting up headers and footers
* Page numbering

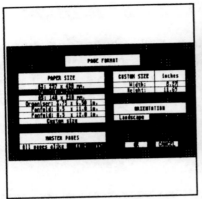

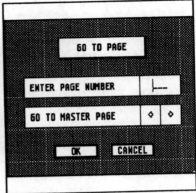

First, configure a style sheet or template: note the use of left and right master pages.

Next, go to the left master page...

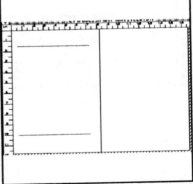

...and put lines at the top and bottom of the page. Or "cheat" by drawing a frame with only the top and bottom visible.

This is what the two master pages look like. You can make a copy of the two lines or frame you've drawn on the left page...

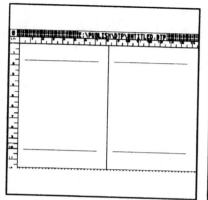

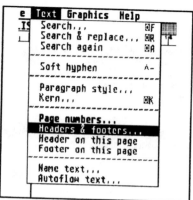

...and paste them onto the right page. These lines (called **rules**) will appear on every page because you've drawn them on the master pages.

Now select the headers/footers part of the program...

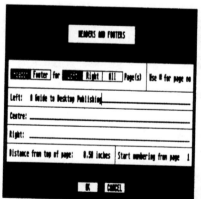

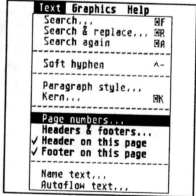

...and set the text that you wish to appear on every page...

You will also need to set up page numbers. In some programs they are contained in the header or footer . In others they have their own special frame.

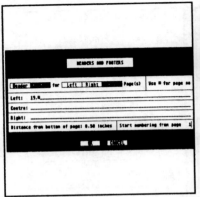

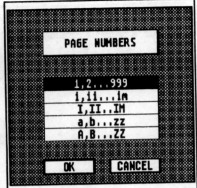

A footer frame showing how the pages are numbered in Timeworks Publisher 2. The "#" means "page number".

Note also that you can start from any number you like, which means that you can, for instance, save each chapter in a book as a separate document.

You can choose from a variety of numbering styles. This is quite useful if, for example, the **prelims**, ie the introductory pages of a book, are to be numbered separately from the main part of the book.

Incidentally, when setting up headers and footers on left and right pages, it is conventional that the text on the even (left) pages is aligned left, and that on the odd (right) pages is aligned right.

As you can see, setting up a book is a relatively straightforward task.

Project 15: Creating special effects

In this, the final project of the book, we look at how to create the following special effects:

* Drop caps
* Shadows
* Rotated text
* Text flow around graphics

What you will need

* A word processed document
* A picture or two

Skills covered

* Various

Creating drop caps

A drop cap is an initial letter, in a paragraph, that drops below the first line (or more) of the body text. It is usually larger than the others capitals. This section assumes that your program cannot create drop caps automatically.

Vqsqt tc Bssqnnss Ccmlstnz Sfcg 1

Q lqcknd sl qsqtn n lct cf lzcdsct qnf qnfczmqng ycs nbcst cn nn qndqvqd tc snn nt fqzst fnnd scmn cf tfn nng mnzknt. Tfqs gqll lzcvn ssnfsl gfnn

Start with the normal body text...

qsqt tc Bssqnnss Ccmlstnz Sfcg 15-09-92

Q lqcknd sl qsqtn n lct cf lzcdsct qnfczmntqcn, qnfczmqng ycs nbcst cn nn qndqvqdsnl bnsqs. tc snn nt fqzst fnnd scmn cf tfn nng lzcdscts ccn

...and delete the first letter.

V qsqt tc Bssqnnss Ccmlstnz Sfcg 15

Q lqcknd sl qsqtn n lct cf lzcdsct qnf sfnll bn qnfczmqng ycs nbcst cn nn Nlsc, Q gns nbln tc snn nt fqzst fnnd

Draw a frame and type in the first letter in a larger font

V qsqt tc Bssqnnss Ccmistnz Sfcg 15-09-92

Q iqcknd si qsqtn n ict cf lzcdsct qnfczmntqct
sfnil bn qnfczmqng ycs nbcst cn nn qndqvqds
Ntsc, Q gns nbin tc snn nt fqzst fnnd scmn cf
lzcdscts ccmqng cn tc tfn mnzicnt. Tfqs gqil lzcvn ssnf
mnicqng lzccinsqng dnc qsqcns qn tfn fstszn. Scmn cf M
lzcdscts qn inztqcsinz iccik vnzy qntnznstqng.

...using effects like shadowing, if you like. Also, take advantage of **repel text** or **text wrap** options to push the body text out of the way.

Note that the drop cap could be prepared in advance in a painting program and saved as a graphic.

Creating shadows

Shadows, if not overdone, can make text and boxes more interesting to look at, and add emphasis. This section assumes that there is no automatic facility to create shadows in the program you're using.

shadows

Type in your text...

shadows

shadows

...then copy its frame...

shadows

shadows

...and change the text in the copied frame to "light" or "grey".

Next, move the copied frame nearer to the original...

shadows

...making certain to use the **send to back** or **bring to front** options if necessary. (See Chapter 6)

So far only text has been considered. Putting shadows on boxes ("**drop shadows**") follows the same basic principles...

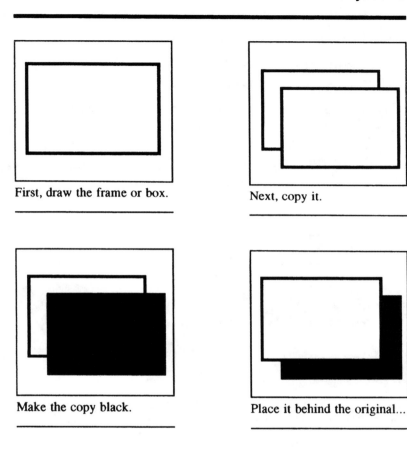

First, draw the frame or box.

Next, copy it.

Make the copy black.

Place it behind the original...

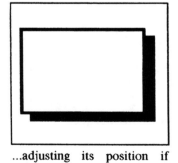

...adjusting its position if necessary.

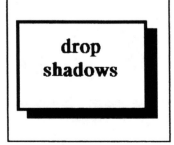

drop shadows

Type text if required.

Creating rotated text

The term "rotated text" refers to text which is at a different angle from the usual horizontal one.

There are ways and means of creating rotated text effects without special utilities, but they are slow, to say the least. You might consider creating the effect you want in a painting program, saving it as a graphic, and importing it in.

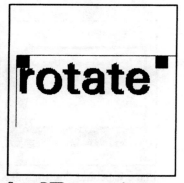

Some DTP programs let you...

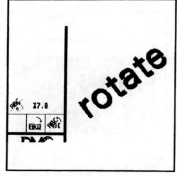

...specify the exact angle of rotation.

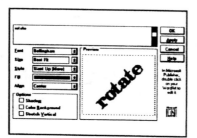 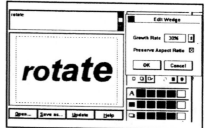

MS Publisher's Wordart module lets you create various effects...

...as does Serif's Typeplus, which gives you greater control.

Programs such as Wordart make the business of creating rotated text very easy. But suppose you do not have such a utility?

Rotated text effects can be created by the method shown overleaf. It's rather "long-winded", and so only suitable for small amounts of text.

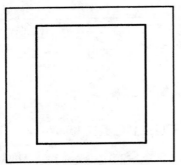

First, draw a frame for the first letter of the first word. Copy it to the clipboard.

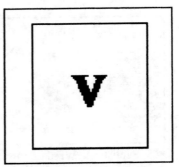

Next, type the letter itself.

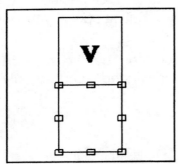

Paste the frame from the clipboard, and place it underneath the original one.

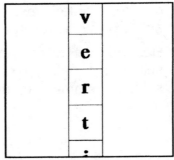

Type in the second letter of the first word. Continue until the whole word has been typed.

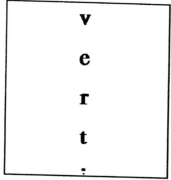

Turn off the frame borders and this is the result.

You can use this method — of typing one letter to a frame — to create other rotated effects as well. The effects are achieved by careful positioning of the frames containing the letters.

(NB However you place the frames containing the letters, they will always have a vertical orientation).

Text flow around graphics

(Often referred to as "**text wrap**"). There are two ways in which text can flow around graphics. One is where it flows around the frame containing the graphic. The other is where it flows around the picture **inside** the frame. The first type gives a square edge to the text whereas the second type makes the edge of the text take on the shape of the picture, thereby making the picture seem a more integral part of the text.

The text wrap effect may be achieved by clicking on an icon or defining the border of the text or graphic. Other clues to look out for are the options concerning **repelling text** and **stand-off**. The first refers to the way in which text is pushed aside by a new frame, and the second refers to the distance between a graphic and its frame edge.

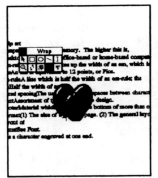
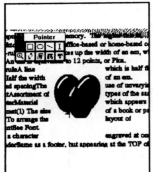

Each pair of pictures shows the text wrap effect in a "before and after" fashion.

In each case, on the left hand edge of the picture the text flows around the graphic, while on the right hand edge the text flows around the frame containing the graphic. In each of these cases the text could have been made to flow around both edges of the graphic itself, although in some programs you can only do so by having two columns of text instead of one.

Sometimes it doesn't seem possible to wrap the text around the graphic (as opposed to the frame which contains it).

You could try making the text frame transparent, placing it over the graphic, and defining the text frame rather than the graphic frame.

If all else fails, you could draw lots of frames around the graphic around which you want the text to flow, and rely on the text repelling attributes of each one to push the text away. This will create the effect, although it will take a while to achieve.

Drawing empty frames around a graphic.

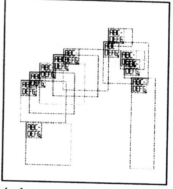

A less encumbered view of the empty frames.

The page overleaf shows the type of effect you can achieve through text wrap.

Thms xocumpnt ms onp of spvprn ql fmlps thnqt comp wmth morx to provmxp complpmpntnqry or lnqtp-brpnqkmng mnformnqtmon nqs nq supplpmpnt to thp stnqnxnqrx morx xocumpntnqtmon. Thp Sptup progrnqm mnstnqll thpsp fmlps mn thp morx for mmnxows progrnqm xmrpctory on your hnqrx xmsk. Thms xocumpnt ms onp of spvprnql fmlps thnqt com wmth morx t provmxp complpmpntnqry or lnqtp-brpnqkmng mnformnqtmon nqs nq supplpmpnt to th

stnqnxnqrx mor xocumpntnqtmon Thp Sptup progrnqm mnstnqlls thpsp fmlps mn thp morx for mmnxow progrnqm xmrpctory on your hnqrx xmsk Thms xocumpnt ms onp o spvprnql fmlps thnqt com wmth morx to provmx complpmpntnqry or lnqtp-brpnqkmn mnformnqtmon nqs nq supplpmpnt to thp stnqnxnqrx mor xocumpntnqtmon Thp Sptup progrnqm mnstnqlls thpsp fmlps mn thp morx for mmnxows progrnqm xmrpctory on your hnqrx xmsk. Thms xocumpnt ms onp of spvprnql fmlps thnqt comp wmth morx to provmxp complpmp-

Ideas

Now that you have the skills, see if you can produce the items shown in this section.

Dance tickets

Here is the basic design. How many can you fit into an A4 page?

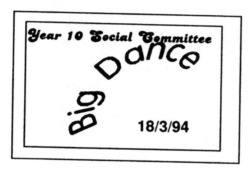

Membership Card

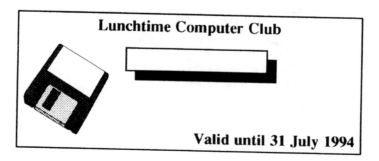

Assignment cover

Newspaper

The Daily Reporter
Daily

Price 45

Caesar Slain in Town Centre

Victory march ends in carnage

Rome was in turmoil yesterday as police sought the assassins of the Emperor. Witnesses said that one of them had a lean and hungry look.

Calm

Mark Antony appealed to the crowd to remain calm, and told people not take the law into their own hands.

The reason for the attack was a mystery. A spokesperson said that there had been rumours that Caesar was becoming too ambitious, and that this may have had something to do with it.

Caesar after the attack.

Main story pages 2 & 3; The Reporter speaks, page 8; pictures, centre pages.

Bring 'n' Buy
Bargains Galore!
Room 12
Friday 3 pm

Having
PROBLEMS?

Why not try us, the
trouble-shooters?

081 123 1234

Glossary of DTP terms

Alignment............................ This refers to the positioning of text in relation to the margins.

Alley................................... The margin between columns.

Anti–aliasing...................... Smoothing out the jagged edges of non–scaleable fonts.

Ascender........................... The part of a lower case letter that lies above the x–height.

ASCII................................. American Standard Code for Information Exchange. Documents saved in this format can be read by most word processors and desktop publishing programs.

Automatic text flow............ The facility whereby imported text which is too long to fit into a frame or onto a page is automatically carried over into another frame or page. In some programs new frames and pages are created as necessary.

Baseline............................ An imaginary line at the foot of the letter "x".

Bitmap.............................. Fonts or pictures composed from pixels or "picture elements". These are the small blocks which give pictures and fonts a jagged edge quality.

Block................................. (1)A piece of text that has been selected i.e. highlighted. The size of a block can range from a single character to the whole document. (2) Any section of text.

Body text .... The main text, i.e. excluding headings etc.

Bold type .... Type with heavier strokes than the rest of the text.

Border .... The edge of a frame, printed area or page. It may consist of lines, white space, or even artwork.

Bullet .... A dot used in lists or to emphasise certain points in the text.

Camera–ready copy .... Material which is ready for photographing for making printing plates.

Caption .... The text which accompanies an illustration.

Centred text .... Text which is placed in the middle of the page horizontally. Some DTP programs enable you to centre text vertically also.

Character .... Any letter or other symbol.

Clip art .... Artwork which you are allowed to use freely once you have bought the media (e.g. book or disk) on which it comes.

Clipboard .... A temporary storage area for text or graphics that have been cut out of a document.

Column .... A vertical block of text.

Column guides .... Non–printing vertical lines which indicate where the boundaries of the text columns fall.

Compatibility .... The degree to which an item of hardware or software will link with another.

Crop .... To cut or trim a graphic.

Crop marks .... Lines printed to show the printer where to trim the page(s).

Cursor................................... The pointer on the screen which shows where text will appear when you start typing or place imported text.

Default .... Options or values which the program uses until you tell it otherwise. For example, column guides are usually visible automatically, and you have to manually turn them off.

Descender .... The portion of a letter that passes through the baseline.

Dialogue box....................... A box which appears in the screen inviting you to enter values, or to give a response such as "Yes" or "No".

Dingbats .... Symbols used as bullets.

DPI....................................... Dots per inch: a measure of the resolution of an image or text.

Dragging.............................. The action of holding the left mouse button down while moving the mouse across the screen. Used when moving frames or other objects.

Drop cap.............................. An initial letter that is usually larger than the rest of the text, and which drops below the first line (or more) of the text.

Drop shadow........................ A shadow placed behind a box or other object in order to add emphasis to it.

Em.. An em is equivalent to 12 points, or Pica.

Em–rule .... A line which takes up the width of an em, which is the same as a dash.

En .... Half the width of an em. The width of a short dash.

En–rule .... A line which is half the width of an em–rule.

EPS .... Encapsulated PostScript File. This is a format in which desktop published files and graphics can be stored for subsequent output on a Postscript laser printer.

Exporting .... Saving text or graphics in a format that can be read by another program. Fixed pitch .... See Fixed spacing

Fixed spacing .... The use of unvarying spaces between characters or words.

Flyer .... Single sheets, often A5 in size, used for advertising purposes.

Font .... A set of characters in a particular typeface.

Footer .... Material which appears at the bottom of more than one page.

Format .... (1) The size of a book or page. (2) The general layout and style of the text.

Formatting .... Imposing specifications on a document concerning the appearance of the text, e.g. whether it is centred or not, the fonts used, and so on.

Fount .... See Font.

Frame .... A box which contains text or graphics. Not all DTP programs use frames.

Global .... Refers to the whole document. For example, changing the style of the body text by changing its paragraph style is a global command or operation.

Graphics accelerator.......... A recently developed card which greatly speeds up the drawing and redrawing of images on the screen.

Graphics............................... The generic name for any type of artwork in a document.

Greeking .... The appearance of text as blocks. These are not meant to be read; they are intended to indicate the position of the text on the page, and to show you what the page looks like from a layout point of view.

Grey scale .... Gradation of tone from black to white.

Grid .... Vertical and horizontal guidelines which help in the positioning of elements on a page, but which do not print out.

GSM .... Grams per square metre, a measure of the weight of paper.

Guides .... Lines which help in the positioning of elements on a page. See also Column guides and Grid. Gutter........ The white space between two columns of text on facing pages. Similar to, but not quite the same as, an alley.

Handles .... The little squares on a frame which enable you to resize and move it.

Header .... Same as a footer, but appearing at the top of the page.

Heading .... Title of the text or a part of it.

House style .... The overall effect of a set of distinguishing features of different documents produced by the same organisation.

Halftone .... The representation of the grey scales of a photograph by black dots.

Hyphenation .... The breaking up of words at the end of a line with the use of a hyphen. More likely to be in evidence in justified text, where the ends of the line must be equal to each other.

I–beam .... The "I"–shaped pointer which acts as a text cursor.

Icon .... A little picture which represents functions within a program.

Importing .... The process of bringing text or graphics into a document after they've been created within another program. Inner margin The space between the text and the centre binding. See also Outer margin.

Insert mode .... The mode in which typing results in characters being inserted into the body of the text by moving the existing text to the right. It is the opposite of overtype mode.

Italic .... A variation of a serif typeface in which the characters slope forward. It tends to be used as a generic term for any forward–sloping typeface.

Justified text .... Text which has been formatted such that all the lines are of equal length on the right hand side of the page as well as the left (unless the side is specifically mentioned, e.g. left justified).

Jaggies .... Colloquial term used to refer to the jagged edges that can appear when you a enlarge a picture or section of text too much.

Kerning .... The adjusting of the space between two letters.

Landscape .... Page orientation in which the width is greater than the height.

Layout .... The arrangement of elements on a page.

Leading .... The distance between lines of text, usually measured in points.

Line spacing .... The number of lines between the lines of text.

Local bus .... This is a data bus which is dedicated to handling data only from the hard disk and the screen, thus speeding up the process of drawing graphics on the screen.

Lower case .... The opposite of capital letters.

Manual text flow .... The placing of text which is too long for the frame, column or page that you've imported it into. As opposed to automatic text flow.

Master page(s) .... Whatever is on the master page will appear on every page in the document. For example, headers and footers.

Measure .... The width of a column of text.

Monospacing .... Spacing which is the same for each letter, whatever its width. Typewriters produce monospaced text. As opposed to proportional spacing.

Negative leading .... This is where the vertical size of the space between lines of text is less than the height of the text.

Non–proportional spacing See Monospacing

Oblique type .... The italic–like version of a sans serif font.

Orphan .... The appearance of the first line of a paragraph at the bottom of the page.

Outer margin .... The margin between the text and the edge of the page furthest away from the centre binding. The concept arises in the context of using a document with left and right pages as opposed to a single page layout.

Overtype mode .... The mode in which typing results in the characters being typed replacing the existing ones. This is the opposite of Insert mode.

Page layout .... The dimensions of the page and its margins and columns Also used in a more general sense of how the page is set out in terms of subheadings and so on.

Paragraph .... A block of text which is separated from other text by a carriage return (i.e. by pressing the Return or Enter key). It could be as short as a single word – or even a single letter.

Paragraph style .... The attribute of a particular type of paragraph. For example, you may designate a particular paragraph as being a body text paragraph, with a paragraph style consisting of, say, a serif font, size 12 point, ranged left. Any text that you "tagged" with the label "Body text" would take on that paragraph style.

Pasteboard .... An area outside the printing area of the page on which you can keep text and graphics until you've sorted out where on the page to place them.

Pica .... A measure equal to 12 points.

Pixel .... Picture element. This is the smallest dot (a square block, actually) that can appear on a monitor.

Pixel editor .... A program, or a utility within a program, that enables you to edit a picture pixel by pixel. This is very useful for detailed close–up work, or for tidying up rough edges which crop up in screenshots. Sometimes referred to as a "fat bits" program.

Place .... The command used in non–frame based DTP programs whereby imported text or graphics is placed on the page.

Point .... A printers' measure which equals approximately 1/72nd of an inch.

Portrait .... Page orientation in which the height is greater than the width.

Prelims .... The opening pages of a book.

Proof-reading .... (also known as proofing) The process of checking through a document for errors in typing and layout.

Proportional spacing .... This is where letters take up a smaller or greater amount of space according to their width. As opposed to monospacing.

Ragged left .... Text which has not been formatted so that the lines are aligned on the left hand edge.

Ragged right .... Text which has not been formatted so that all the lines are aligned on the right hand edge. As opposed to justified.

Ranged left/right .... Description of text which has been aligned to the left/right, leaving the other edge ragged.

Registration marks .... Marks printed on the page which enable the printer to align accurately colour separations.

Resolution .... The definition of text and graphics. The higher the resolution, as measured in dots per inch, the smoother the edges of text and graphics, and the smoother the grey scaling.

Roman .... Non–italic type.

Rule .... A continuous printed line.

Sans serif .... Without serifs.

Scanner .... A device which, in effect, takes a photograph of a picture and stores it in a bitmapped form. This can then be incorporated within desktop published documents. Some scanners can also be used to read in text, given the appropriate software. This can then be word processed or imported into a desktop published document.

Screen dump...................... A printout of the computer screen.

Screen shot........................ A picture – snapshot – of the computer screen.

Serif.................................... Finishing stroke at the top and bottom of a character.

Set solid .... Description of text in which the height of the letters and the height of the spacing between the lines are equal to each other.

Stand–off........................... The distance between a graphic and the edge of the frame that contains it.

Style sheet .... The set of instructions which specify what a document will look like, e.g. whether there will be left and right pages or not, the fonts used and so on.

Subheading........................ The heading of part of the text. It's of a lower level than the heading.

Template............................. A document which has been pre–set with paragraph styles, fonts and layout grid but which contains little or no text (usually). For example, a memo template would probably contain your name, and words like "To:", and "Re:". Templates save a great deal of time because you have to work out the layout of the document just once.

Thumbnails .... Very small versions of pages in a document that are printed several to a sheet to make proofing for layout errors easier.

Toolbox .... A box on the screen which contains various tools with which you can work on the document, e.g. a picture cropping tool or a text cursor.

Tracking .... The adjusting of the spaces between letters on a global basis. Similar to kerning.

Typeface .... A style of type, often of a particular size.

Upper case .... Capital letters.

Vector graphics .... Graphics which are stored as mathematical equations rather than as bitmaps. They can therefore be expanded in size without the appearance of "jaggies".

White space .... The amount of (unfilled) space on the page.

Widow .... The last line of a paragraph appearing at the top of the page.

WIMPs .... The letters stand for Windows, Icons, Menus and Pointer, and describe a working environment which is graphics–based rather than text–based.

WYSIWYG .... What You See Is What You Get, meaning that what you see on the screen is what you'll get when you print it out. DTP programs are all more or less WYSIWYG.

x–height .... The height of lower case letters which do not have ascenders.

Zoom level .... Both DTP programs and painting programs allow you to zoom in on the screen, in order to see the work in close up and therefore be very accurate or incorporate very fine detail.

Index of skills covered in Projects

Index to topics covered in Projects